# TANDEM
# TALES

# TANDEM TALES

## OR
## "For Better and For Worse
## For Uphill and For Downhill
## As Long As We Both
## Shall Pedal"

## MICHAEL BATTISTI

iUniverse, Inc.
Bloomington

## TANDEM TALES

*or "For Better and For Worse For Uphill and For Downhill*
*As Long As We Both Shall Pedal"*

*iUniverse books may be ordered through booksellers or by contacting:*

*iUniverse*
*1663 Liberty Drive*
*Bloomington, IN 47403*
*www.iuniverse.com*
*1-800-Authors (1-800-288-4677)*

*ISBN: 978-1-4620-5757-3 (sc)*
*ISBN: 978-1-4620-5758-0 (ebk)*

*Printed in the United States of America*

*iUniverse rev. date: 10/22/2011*

*She put my ring on her finger*

*Her feet on the pedals*

*And her life in my hands*

## To Stephanie

"As we passed on, it seemed as if those scenes of visionary enchantment would never have an end"

—Meriwether Lewis

# CONTENTS

# INTRODUCTION

The ultimate compatibility test: riding with your spouse across the United States on a tandem bicycle. We had been warned:

"Riding a tandem bike will make or break your marriage."

"Some people just need to be the captain of their own ship (or bike)."

But after 30 years of marriage, my wife, Stephanie, and I decided to throw all caution to the wind. We quit our jobs, and leaving our house in care of our children, set out on the biggest adventure of our lives.

It all started innocently enough. My wife and I were having a hard time finding some type of outdoor recreation that we could enjoy together due to our difference in abilities. We hiked, skied, and kayaked at different speeds. We even tried sailing but Stephanie got seasick on our little Sunfish. Then twenty plus years after leaving our bikes to rust in the garage we acquired some tag-sale bikes and began cycling (actually my wife's bike had disappeared, we believed it was pawned off by her brother Bobby who was in need of some cash). We both enjoyed our outings, but Stephanie still felt guilty about my having to wait up for her occasionally.

A couple of summers later, I found myself with some free time and began working a few hours each week at a local bike shop. Guy, the owner, learning of our predicament, suggested that we try a used tandem that he had out back. "Take her home and go for a spin. If things don't work out, you can bring it back."

The first attempts at just getting on our saddles in unison were quite comical (performed on our side yard—grass is much less abrasive on flesh than pavement). After the first few attempts ended with one of us on the ground, the next several (announced by my "ready—one—two—three") were aborted by her response, "NO! I'M NOT READY!" Once over the initial fear however, we soon had the starting and stopping synchronized, and found ourselves flying down the roads having a grand time! The exhilarating downhill speeds generated by the weight of the tandem far exceeded what we were accustomed to on our single bikes; we felt as if we were on a runaway freight train. Also we were now arriving at the top of each climb together. We were hooked.

By the following summer, our daily forays were getting longer and longer. We rode to visit friends, county parks, and our favorite diners and ice cream shops. And as the grand finale of the cycling season, we signed up to take a six-day supported tour of Nova Scotia with an established touring company. During this ride, Stephanie and I made many new friends, enjoyed the local fare, and explored the scenic province at a leisurely pace (with the added satisfaction that we had done it under our own power). We yearned for more. With this experience under our belts, the seed was planted to do a longer, self-supported tour.

We had to wait several more years until the time was right. After working our family farm near Syracuse, New York for almost 30 years, we had decided to sell the farm to our herdsman. It had been a difficult transaction to swallow, as it had been in the family since 1869. But our four children had all grown up, without any desire to commit to the hardships and long hours of a dairy and maple farm. We headed north, where the lure of the Adirondack Mountains had enticed us to spend many of our vacations over the years (yes, some farmers do get vacations).

We had no trouble finding jobs as we settled into a rented cottage in Essex, perched on a bluff overlooking impressively large Lake Champlain. There our love of tandem cycling grew. We toured around the lake, incorporating its multiple ferries to create loops along both the New York and Vermont shores and Champlain's northern Hero Islands. With its mix of farms and orchards against the backdrop of the Adirondack and Green Mountains, the Champlain Valley's scenery was tough to beat. We found ourselves the recipients of much attention; the novelty of riding "a bicycle built for two" brought many compliments, questions, and comments (the number one being, "she's not pedaling back there!"). Soon the desire to take an extended, two-wheeled adventure was stronger than ever, and when a friend asked, "doing anything special for your upcoming 30th wedding anniversary?" we knew it was just the excuse we needed to commit to a big trip. And by this time we had decided to go all out, and shoot for a transcontinental trip—from the Atlantic to the Pacific!

In the fall before our departure, now living in Jay, New York, Stephanie and I took advantage of a beautiful Indian Summer weekend in the Adirondacks to do a "shake-down" tour with our equipment. Riding between campgrounds in the neighboring communities of Wilmington and Saranac Lake (near the Olympic village of Lake Placid) we put our fully-loaded bike to the test. It handled like a charm, although I definitely felt that over the winter I needed to modify the stock gearing that came with the bike so we could crawl up steep grades a little easier.

Over the winter some of the logistical problems on the home front were solved. Our daughter Melanie and son-in-law Ken announced that they would be moving back to the east coast from California with our first grandchild Elijah and agreed to help our youngest Zachary house sit for us. Also our son Andrew learned he would be heading to West Virginia (in the general direction of our starting point in Yorktown, Virginia) in May for a summer internship and could transport us and our gear on his way.

When it came time to select our route, we turned to the Adventure Cycling Association for help. Being big fans and members of the non-profit organization (whose mission is to promote bicycle travel by the development and mapping of cycling routes) we decided to follow portions of two of their more popular routes: the TransAmerica and the Northern Tier. The ACA publishes highly detailed maps of these routes and others, denoting all services pertinent to the touring cyclist. Santa left Stephanie the complete set of maps under our Christmas tree that year (along with a case of "butt butter"—many long distance cyclists' saving grace).

The TransAm Route is to the cyclist as the Appalachian Trail is to the hiker: the granddaddy of all North American routes, starting in Yorktown, Virginia and ending in Astoria, Oregon. We would divert from it in Missoula, Montana and head north to intercept the Northern Tier in Libby, Montana. The Northern Tier is also a transcontinental route, stretching from Bar Harbor, Maine to Anacortes, Washington. From Libby we would follow it west, exiting in Rockport, Washington just shy of the Pacific Ocean. Then turning due south, we would follow a self-mapped route to Seattle.

Having never been to many of the states that we would pass through, Stephanie and I would be given an education around every bend. The road would be our classroom and we would learn about each state's people, history, agriculture, and geography. It would be a voyage of enlightenment that no textbook could match. Finishing in Seattle, we would be assured a hero's welcome and hospitality before flying back home, as I had three brothers and a sister and their families living in the Emerald City.

In late winter we officially gave notice to our employers. We both enjoyed our jobs, but felt they were expendable for such a once-in-a-lifetime opportunity. Our friends and family were very supportive, although some thought us crazy (and my father-in-law still insists that we went about it all wrong—an RV or a motorcycle was the only way to go cross-country).

About one month before our departure date, Stephanie came home from work and announced that we should ride for a cause, so being a National Public Radio junkie, I pledged support for our local affiliate. Stephanie followed suit with support for public television as to insure grandson Elijah would continue to be treated to Sesame Street. As the pledges began to roll in (per mile), we knew there would be no way to back out now.

# CHAPTER 1

# EQUIPMENT AND LOGISTICS

## The Bike

Our bike was a steel-framed Burley "Duet" Tandem which handled extremely well fully-loaded. Unfortunately, Burley no longer makes bikes, only their popular trailers. The rear wheel's hub was threaded to accept an Arai drum break (common with tandems), essential for keeping the speed of a fully-loaded tandem under control on long, steep descents. Some tandems with stock rim brakes have eyelets on the frame to mount a disc brake for the same purpose. I put the lever for this brake on Stephanie's handlebars to give her something to do, as I did all the regular braking and shifting up front. She's a control freak and I had to give her credit for sitting back and putting her life in my hands for three months. She also had a rear-view mirror to better view the coal and logging trucks bearing down on us, and a ding-a-ling bell to awaken any dogs that might be sleeping through the opportunity of chasing a passing cyclist. Her handlebars somewhat resembled the "Busy Box" we remember hanging off the side of our cribs when we were babies.

I mentioned earlier my concern for lower gearing after our shakedown tour. Newer bikes now have interchangeable sprockets, or "cassettes" that will allow one to lower his or her gearing without a major investment. I replaced ours with cassette containing a larger "granny gear." However, ones bike will need to have a "long cage rear derailleur" to accept this. Check with your local bike shop if you're in doubt. I also modified the "triple" chain rings (the set of three gears down by your pedals—if you're bike only has two, you'll be sorry unless you're superhuman or planning on just doing the tour of Kansas). I replaced the smallest of these three chainrings with an even smaller one, giving us additional lower gearing. This did create

1

a big jump down from our middle chainring, so I installed a "chain watcher," a guide which insures the chain won't derail when shifting. This new combination of gears required a long chain, and I made sure that the bike shifted safely in each extreme combination. Again, obtain the services of a competent bike mechanic if necessary. These relatively inexpensive alterations greatly lowered our gearing and allowed us to sustain momentum on all but the steepest grades when fully loaded.

## Gear and How We Carried It

One of the challenges of two people touring on a single bike is the limited cargo capacity. Except for what can be stowed in a tandem-specific frame bag (which hangs in the portion of the bike frame in front of the rear rider or "stoker"), there is no room for any more panniers than what a single bike could be outfitted with. A trailer could be employed. However, I pulled the plug on that option, rationalizing that a tandem was awkward enough to park and maneuver without the additional length of a trailer. Besides, I didn't want to encourage Stephanie to bring along even more "necessities." Before the trip, she wrote in her journal, "I have done a trial packing of my bike bags with the clothes I want to bring along and it weighed in at twelve pounds. Mike told me to thin them out. Either that or we will be mailing some home after the first big hill. I'm packing for a three month journey and he expects me to bring only two bike shorts! This should be interesting!"

We packed as if we were "ultra-light" campers. Use the best gear you can afford. The new stuff is much lighter and functional. I invested $300 in a new MSR Hubba Hubba tent, which we loved. It paid for itself, as I was able to get my wife to camp more (and "hotel" less) than if we had my old backpacking tent, which had only one door and was like climbing into a banana peel.

We employed four panniers, one handlebar bag, one under-the-seat "wedge" bag, and the fore-mentioned tandem-specific frame bag on our voyage. Our tent and sleeping pads were stacked on top of the rear panniers. Because our front panniers were full-sized (most touring cyclists use a smaller set for the front) I invested in a heavy duty front rack. It mounted much more securely than most, using the axle skewer instead of small screws. To save weight and room we did not bring any cooking gear. We did carry cold food and/or snacks, but we generally stopped at a diner to have a hearty breakfast and dinner at each end of the day.

## Bike Shop Availability

Or lack of it. Yes, we did travel on an established bike route, but it travels mainly through SMALL TOWNS, to avoid heavy traffic. Shops were far and few between. Have your bike checked over thoroughly before leaving. BE PREPARED to handle common repairs yourself. Carry spare parts, tubes, a tire, and tools and know how to use them. If you're not confident in your abilities, many bike shops offer courses in basic bike maintenance and adjustment (including puncture repair). Do preventative maintenance on a regular basis before and DURING your voyage—tightening bolts, lubing the chains, checking brake pads, and most importantly topping off your tires with air. Because of the extra weight stress put upon tandem wheels, I got into the habit of checking them each day when we reached our destination; lifting each wheel off the ground and giving it a spin to check for any wobbles, and then yanking it side to side to check for any bearing play. Also, keep in mind that a tandem is moving two people with the same gauge drive chain that a single bike moves one person with, so use quality chains and take good care of them. Have them checked for stretch periodically and changed them before they break and/or inflict premature wear on your cassette! Spinning in a low gear (high RPM's) instead of hammering in a high one will also do wonders for the longevity of your chains, gears, and knees.

## Training

During the winter preceding our trip, Stephanie took a spin class at the local gym and I did a lot of cross-country skiing (cross training). When spring arrived (and it comes late in the Adirondacks—the saying goes we have nine months of winter and three months of poor sledding) it was cold and difficult to get motivated to begin riding. Nonetheless, we did get in many sorties in May, but we didn't over-do it, remembering that this was supposed to be fun. We felt were in good shape when we started, and most importantly our butts were accustomed to and comfortable on our saddles of choice for

EXTENDED PERIODS (we had experimented with several brands during the last few seasons).

## Monetary Matters

We received this email from my Aunt and Uncle a month into the trip:

> "We read recently in one of our engineering magazines that a cyclist can travel 12 mph with an effort comparable to walking. Also, one can cycle about 1000 miles at 15 mph using the amount of energy comparable to 1 gallon of gasoline. So I guess you are using the equivalent of four gallons of gas or about $10.40 worth of fossil fuel to go across America. Of course, I guess you have to add in the price of a few burgers and chocolate milkshakes. Keep it up, Phil and Jean."

Yes, we saved on gas by cycling, but by traveling at such a relatively slow rate of speed we spent over 90 days on the road, and the expense of all those burgers and shakes (and campsites and motels) did add up. We averaged over $100 per day in expenses for the two of us, but we camped only 56% of the nights (only 42% in the east, where it was hot and muggy and tough to get a good-night's sleep without air-conditioning). Obviously, by utilizing more make-shift camping opportunities (i.e. church lawns and village greens—many with limited or non-existing facilities) and preparing your own meals (with the added weight of cooking gear) one could reduce this expense considerably.

## Support for the UN-Supported Touring Cyclists

We resupplied with several "mail drops" on our journey. Before we left, anything we couldn't risk being without and thought we might not be able to find (or at least not in an economically sized package) was stockpiled. Handy items such as sample-size bottles of shampoo and toothpaste, zip-lock bags of powered laundry detergent (later we discovered soap impregnated "laundry sheets"), our size tires and tubes, maps, Gatorade powder, medications, and plenty of tubes of butt butter were organized out on the workbench of our garage. Then later, at our request, our children would mail us these items, safely packed for shipment with wads of the local newspaper (which made for great reading, keeping us abreast of the news back home in Jay).

The trick with mail drops was to time your arrival at the chosen post office as soon as possible (especially if we were out of butt butter) but not before unless you wished to take an unscheduled "zero day" waiting for the package to arrive (or a weekend off if arriving after high noon on a Saturday). We also learned to avoid mailing to large cities, as it was much easier to find a post office in a town that had no more than a blinking red light (although in this day and age it may be wise to call ahead to small-town post offices to make sure they haven't been boarded up by the federal government).

## Why East to West? Or the "Direction Dilemma"

Most people's first instincts would tell them to follow the general direction of the prevailing winds across the United States and cycle west to east to make use of headwinds. However, there are several other factors to take into consideration:

1. Leaving in May on the west coast risks encounters with snow and cold weather in the passes of the Cascades and Rockies
2. Cycling west to east early in the morning entails riding with the sun in your eyes (and in the eyes of motorists trying to pass you)
3. We prefer to ride in the morning (when winds, temperatures, humidity and traffic were the least troublesome) and didn't want that sun in our eyes!

And as most cyclists soon discover, these "westerly prevailing winds" are not as prominent on the ground as on a weather map.

## Dogs

A big debate exists among touring cyclists over the weapon(s) of choice when encountering the more sporting ones. We had great luck with a whistle that Stephanie would blow at approaching canines. She wore it around her neck for quick access. For insurance, I carried a canister of pepper spray in my jersey pocket (but we never used it). I think the fact that there were two of us on one bike either confused or intimidated some of the dogs. In conversations with fellow cyclists, we learned of many other creative weapons, including squirts of water, the water bottle itself, tire pumps, and imitations of Darth Vader's breathing.

Kentucky and Missouri have the worst reputation as far as mean dogs go, but were we ever caught off guard when one jumped us in the state of Washington!

## Special Concerns for the Female Partner

When we started in Virginia, Stephanie needed a nice bathroom. By the time we reached Kansas, a big bush (or clump of sunflowers) would do. In Wyoming, I just had to watch for oncoming cars. Then in Everett, Washington, on the overpass leading into the metropolis, I was filled with pride when a three foot high concrete barrier sufficed. She was very adaptable! We found this concern overrated.

## Other Personal Issues

If saddle soreness develops, try making small changes to saddle adjustment, including tilt angle. Rest often and take an occasional day off. And be generous with the butt butter! This cream, worth its weight in gold, reduces friction and soothes tissues made tender by long hours in the saddle. There are several excellent brands available, however some cyclists prefer to use easier-to-find Vaseline or A and D Ointment (but beware—their greasiness is tough to wash out of your shorts—and wash them daily to avoid wearing a lycra Petri dish).

## Miscellaneous Tips

A few tidbits that you may not find in your average bicycle tourist's handbook (which there are several excellent ones in print, which delve into the ABC's of bicycle touring much more thoroughly, and which this book does not attempt to be):

1.  Water quality and quantity is important. Avoid questionable water and/or be prepared to purify it. We couldn't believe

the amount of liquid we went through in the hills and heat! Especially in the East with its high humidity. In every other bottle we added some Gatorade powder, which prevented leg cramps on all but one day. On hot days, we also found the flavoring would increase our fluid intake of the "bath water" that would be inevitable even with our insulated water bottles and the addition of ice. Besides those four 24 oz water bottles, we also carried a one gallon jug (with a large mouth for ice cubes) which we filled for desolate stretches of roadway.

2. Practice good personal hygiene; there's nothing worse than being sick away from home. Wash your hands before eating. Wash fruit and vegetables. We carried baby wipes and waterless sanitizer.

3. Get into the habit of "early to bed, early to rise." It makes a cyclist's life on the road so much better. Not only will you enjoy the previously mentioned weather benefits by riding early in the day, you'll have more time during and after to explore points of interest. And despite being physically exhausted at the end of each day, Stephanie and I discovered that we sometimes had difficulty falling asleep, perhaps a little anxious about what tomorrow would bring. I found reading a good book would knock me out eventually, while Stephanie resorted to a few hands of Solitaire on her IPOD.

4. Speaking of bedtime, the thought of writing down our memoirs in a journal each night was too much for me. I carried a tiny digital recorder which I dictated into each night while snuggled in my sleeping bag.

5. If you don't use it, loose it! After a few days, reassess your baggage, and send home stuff non-essential to your comfort.

6. If in doubt when and where your next Laundromat may be, wash at least your shorts and jersey while showering. A stomach makes a fine washboard, especially if you have six-pack abs (we wish!). At first my wife refused to hand wash, but eventually she came around. Besides, who wants to spend valuable time sitting in a hot Laundromat? Unless of course you have cold beer to drink and a thunderstorm is brewing! And bring some parachute cord for a clothesline.

The ability to jury-rig one in a motel room without ripping down any light fixtures or curtain rods is the true test of a veteran cyclo-tourist (plus it makes watching HBO a little more challenging through pieces of black Lycra). Sometimes we dried wet clothes on the go, in a mesh bag strapped over the top of our panniers.

7. On our shakedown trip, I discovered that my bike shoes didn't have quite enough volume for my feet, which became slightly swollen from several longer days of riding. I ordered a larger pair to save my toenails on the trip.

8. Have business cards printed up with your contact information, blog address, and charity link to swap with people you meet on your trip. You'll want to keep in touch with all your new friends.

9. If you come away with nothing else from this book, know that there is a more economical way to shave on the road than with those tiny and relatively expensive little cans of shaving cream. We discovered William's Shaving Soap as an alternative, and it worked so well that Stephanie even used it to shave her legs.

10. Speaking of alternatives, don't forget to stock up each morning on the forerunner of today's energy gel packets, the Smucker's Jam assortments, available at your local small-town diner. You'll find them hidden right behind the bottles of ketchup and Tabasco sauce. You know it's going to be a great day when you find a rare peach, cherry, or orange marmalade packet hidden underneath the lackluster strawberry.

# CHAPTER 2

## VIRGINIA

### *Broken at the Breaks*

**Dipping the rear wheel into the Atlantic**

## Day 1, May 24, Yorktown to Glendale, VA, 63 miles

For most cyclists beginning a sea to shining sea crossing of America, the commemorative dipping of the rear wheel into the Atlantic (better known here as the York River) is the first photo op. At the suggestion I rolled my eyes, but Stephanie insisted. I eventually came around, needing somewhere to rinse my cycling shoe of dog excrement (I had literally "gotten off on the wrong foot" stepping out of the car). As Andrew dug through our car-load of gear to find the Canon, we began loading the bike. In a week or two, we would have this down to a routine, but the inaugural packing required some organizational skills; at first we went with "his and hers" panniers but later downgraded our strategy to a co-mingling of "his and hers" zip-lock bags. More important, we were careful to put essential items (like raingear, butt butter, and a picture of our new grandson) accessible on the top.

After double-checking all the nooks and crannies of the car for cell-phone chargers, lip balm, and sunglasses, we hugged our son goodbye. As Andrew disappeared in the general direction of West Virginia (to his summer internship at the Radio Telescope Array in Green Bank), it suddenly hit us: this was not a dream, we were all alone, with 4200 miles of pedaling between us and the Pacific Ocean.

The skies were gloomy as we pedaled up the Colonial Parkway. The ride through Colonial Williamsburg was a little confusing and we had to dodge a few heaps of steaming dung, these courtesy of authentic colonial horses. Was it just me or was there a reoccurring theme beginning here in Virginia?

A few miles down the road we encountered our next challenge. A detour: bridge construction forced us off the parkway and onto a nasty four-lane highway with no shoulder. As cars blew by just inches away at 55 mph, Stephanie and I began to have second thoughts about this hare-brained adventure. But alas, the skies cleared and we soon found ourselves on a quiet, slow-paced bike trail with pulses to match.

The rest of the day went smoothly down quiet country roads, passing many historic southern plantations and civil war battlefields. Thus began my insatiable thirst for local history along the trail, and Stephanie began to roll her eyes and moan "yer killin' me" each time she heard my command to "unclick (from the pedals)" as I pulled up to read yet another roadside historical marker. Being the captain of a tandem did have its benefits!

By late afternoon we had checked in at the Willis Church. It would be the first of several churches we would stay at in the east that offered hostel-like accommodations available for cyclists on the trail. There we waited for Sherrill, a high school classmate of mine and first "trail angel," who lived near Richmond. We had prearranged to meet her, and although it did not occur to us at the time, from this night on we would not see another familiar face on our entire journey until a couple of days from Seattle. Sherrill and her daughter were kind enough to pick us up and treat us to a great dinner. We had a lot of news to catch up on and the evening came to an end way too quickly.

### Day 2, May 25, Glendale to Ashland, VA, 40 miles

Before leaving the church we snacked on bagels and peanut butter. In Elko Stephanie rehydrated with a bottle of "G", which she insisted was not Gatorade but in fact a new sports drink. By late morning, it was spitting rain, so we took in the visitor's center at the Richmond National Battlefield Park while the showers passed. The park commemorated eleven different sites where Civil War battles had been fought, including Cold Harbor, one of America's bloodiest, most lopsided battles. Here Ulysses S. Grant admitted to making his biggest mistake of the war. Thirteen thousand Union casualties were incurred in a hopeless frontal assault against the fortified troops of Confederate General Robert E. Lee.

Some gas station pizza hit the spot for a late lunch. We stopped for the day just outside of Ashland, where our Kampground of America turned out to be adjacent to a busy, noisy interstate. Thank goodness we had remembered to bring our earplugs. We played some cards while at the Laundromat, and Stephanie, now anxious to lighten our load after only two days of riding, boxed up some surplus clothes to mail back home. She quipped, "I guess my fashion sense was out-weighted!"

We learned from other campers that we were one day behind an Adventure Cycling group headed west (the organization also offers guided tours). We were eager to make some acquaintances, but we didn't have much hope of catching these cyclists, as they were supported by a van carrying most of their gear.

## Day 3, May 26, Ashland to Mineral, VA, 53 miles

The excitement and expectations of the voyage continued to build today: at Bumpass we stopped at a general store for lunch, where we picnicked outside on perhaps the world's biggest picnic table. We also had the pleasure of meeting our first fellow cross-country cyclist. Bryan hailed from and started in Long Island and was headed to San Francisco, California. At our "campground" behind the firehouse in Mineral, we learned that he had recently worked in Russia for eight years. He covered an average of 90 miles a day (compared to our goal of 50 miles), so it wasn't going to be a drawn-out relationship.

## Day 4, May 27, Mineral to Charlottesville, VA, 58 miles

The country roads turned into a roller-coaster like ride today, and there was an especially steep and narrow stretch leading up to Monticello. We postponed our visit to Thomas Jefferson's estate until the next day, as we wanted to allot sufficient time to take in all the interpretive tours and exhibits that it had to offer. Soon we were finding our way through the city of Charlottesville, home of the stately University of Virginia. We stopped and asked several people for directions to the Super 8, where Stephanie had made reservations for two nights. Most people just rolled their eyes; apparently there was no easy way to get there (without riding on a busy interstate at rush hour). Finally an EMT, a cyclist himself, noticed us consulting our maps at an intersection. He not only gave us great directions, but tips on what to see and do in town. Later that evening, we saw him at the downtown walking mall, where Stephanie and I had dined alfresco.

## Day 5, May 28, Charlottesville, 0 miles

We used the great public transit system to backtrack up to Thomas Jefferson's home at Monticello. In the front hall hung a set of elk antlers, the only artifact on display from the Lewis and Clark Expedition (of which Jefferson was the driving force behind). The TransAm route intersects with the travels of the Corps of Discovery quite often across the country, and we were looking forward to many more of these encounters. Another highlight at Monticello was the narrated tour of Mulberry Row, where Jefferson's slaves had their own little community.

## Day 6, May 29, Charlottesville to Afton, VA, 34 miles

By picking up a city street map of Charlottesville and plotting an alternate route, we managed to get out of Dodge—avoiding the busier commercialized strips by picking our way through some residential neighborhoods. Near White Hall, we stopped and took some pictures where the quiet country road wound through a beautiful vineyard.

We detoured into Crozet and found some lunch at a Subway. There we enjoyed two subs that the Center of Disease Control would have been proud of. The employee who waited on us put on a new pair of plastic gloves after each and every ingredient!

Just a mile out of town, we were startled when a cyclist appeared from nowhere just behind us! I swear he was hiding in the bushes, ready to pounce on unsuspecting touring cyclists.

"I'm Neil, and I'd be happy to escort you up towards Afton!" he yelled. Being from the area, he threw in a lot of commentary on the way! Unfortunately we understood very little of it over the creak of his rusty chain and the fact that he rode so far ahead of us. He "strongly suggested" that we stop at Chiles Peach Orchard, a very popular farm stand. Stephanie and I shared a fresh strawberry milkshake there while Neil went in to do some serious shopping. During our snack break, we met our first east-bound thru-cyclist who had pulled over upon spotting our fully loaded tandem. "Speed Racer" as we later dubbed him had started in San Francisco 40 days earlier and was carrying all of a water bottle on his carbon-fiber bike. A car behind him was hauling everything else (in cycling jargon this is referred to as providing "SAG"—short for Support and Gear). He was impressed by our load.

Neil soon returned with a large bag. "I've got some goodies in here that I'd like you to take up to the Cookie Lady for me. I'll have to turn off before you get there," he explained. Inside the bag were some peaches, a quart canning jar of apple butter, and about six pounds of newsprint. We felt like pack mules.

Now this cookie lady, June Curry, is a legend amongst the cycle-touring community. We had learned of her unrivaled hospitality during and since the inaugural "BikeCentennial" Event of 1976. In fact, we had planned to stay at her "bike house" that very night. Now we had a delivery for her, a heavy package and unfortunately for us, she lived at the top of a very steep hill. Apparently, she didn't get out much anymore and this was Neil's care package for her. As we approached the bottom of the hill, Neil peeled off, wishing us good tailwinds.

The sign on the cookie lady's door read, "Having a bad day, make yourself at home in the bike house (next door)." Unfortunately, I had already knocked before I read the note, but she appeared, happy to see us, and was grateful of the goodies that we had brought.

She did look a little shaky, and was getting on in years.[1] She apologized for not having the bike house in tip top condition, but urged us to stay anyway. I thanked her and we went down to have a look.

If there were to be a Smithsonian for bicycle touring, this was it! Every square inch of wall space in the bike house was decorated with postcards, newspaper clippings, and knickknacks made from bike parts. There was a rack of autographed jerseys, and a library of photo albums and guest logs. As for accommodating us for the night, all the couches were a little too short to sleep on for our tastes and everything had a very musty smell to it (unfortunately rules were posted against opening any doors and windows as any breeze would have turned the thousands of postcards into a blizzard of 3 x 5 inch snowflakes). After discovering the garden hose cold shower, we debated whether to continue the climb up to the Blue Ridge Parkway where there was a motel (given very low ratings from Neil). Although we decided not stay with June, it was an honor to have met her. Each year the Adventure Cycling Association pays homage to her by awarding the "June Curry Award" to a" generous individual or group encountered during a bicycle tour that makes the cyclotourist's journey easier, or in some cases, even possible, by helping the cyclist through an act of goodwill."

---

[1] We later learned she had suffered a stroke in 2005, but had made a good recovery. When we visited her in 2010, she was 87 years old.

We found the Inn at Afton, with its shredded, undecipherable sign blowing in the wind, at the top of a hill overlooking the entrance to the Parkway. After wheeling the bike into the room panniers and all, I jumped in the shower. Ouch! (Note to self: next time, wear bike helmet in shower, shower head was installed at eye level). When Stephanie got in, I added all of our dirty clothes and some laundry detergent at her feet, sort of like a two-legged Maytag. Unfortunately, she didn't have a spin cycle, so we had to wring them out by hand.

## Day 7, May 30, Afton to Vesuvius, VA, 42 miles

Stephanie referred to today as "the ride from hell!" We climbed along on the Blue Ridge Parkway, pedaling up and down, up and down. We took a break at the visitor's center, where there were some nice exhibits and a restored homesteader's cabin. Also we were given some ice cold sodas and cookies from a young lady who parked in her car by a trailhead, waiting to meet her fiancée who was hiking the Appalachian Trail. He was in the service and had just received word that he was to ship out shortly to Iraq. She was there not only to resupply him, but also to say goodbye.

After our last of many overlooks of the Shenandoah Valley, we exited the parkway and began a hair-raising, hand-numbing three mile descent. Stephanie was squeezing the drum break so hard that we broke a spoke. I installed a temporary "Fiber Fix Spoke" (don't leave home without one). Although we carried replacement spokes, the one that broke couldn't be replaced without removing the drum brake, which required a large socket which I deemed too heavy to carry in our otherwise well-stocked tool bag.

At the bottom of the hill we found Vesuvius and Gertie's Country Store (just off-route) where we had an awesome lunch: Gertie's famous (but top secret recipe) pulled pork BBQ sandwich with coleslaw on top. A few flat miles later we pulled into Mallard Duck Campground, a great bargain at $10. Several very nice couples invited us over to their campfires later and provided us with copious amounts of ice-cold liquid refreshment. They also solved the riddle of the very noisy birds that have been keeping us up a night. Apparently they were not birds at all, but tree frogs.

## Day 8, May 31, Vesuvius to Troutville, VA, 54 miles

After breakfast at a nice café in Lexington, we stopped at a Laundromat and wasted the coolest part of the day washing our clothes. This practice had to stop. We passed on the Memorial Day parade, which was just lining up as we snuck out of town.

After a snack in Buchanan, we got caught in our first shower of the trip, but the sun had reappeared by the time we arrived in Troutville. There we had a fine dinner at Shoney's (for those of you not familiar with this southern establishment— imagine a Denny's but with Barry Manilow piped in for some ambiance. After ordering off the menu, we proceeded to the salad bar, where Stephanie's foraging took her over to the hot buffet line (out of bounds for us) for a huge dollop of macaroni and cheese. After her steak, baked potato, and garlic bread went south, she declared room for dessert and ordered a hot fudge strawberry sundae. Two thirds of her way through that she slid it over to me to finish and made one last pass by the salad bar! I realized we were in need of a lot of calories each day, but tonight there were not enough digits on a calculator to count the calories she had consumed.

## Day 9, June 1, Troutville to Christiansburg, VA, 49 miles

Before leaving Troutville we stopped at the Jiffy Lube where the mechanic produced a large enough socket to remove our drum brake. I was then able to replace the temporary spoke from a few days ago with a real one.

Things seemed to happen in twos today. We crossed the Appalachian Trail twice (and encountered a really grumpy hiker), had two uphill's for every downhill, and I consumed two hotdogs during two different rest breaks.

Riding along the North Fork of the Roanoke River before the uphill into Christiansburg, we rode under what we assumed was a viaduct, a very tall and skinny bridge-like structure. Later we learned that it was known as "the bridge to nowhere," completed in 2002 at the cost of 17 million dollars. It is a "transportation research facility" that is eventually supposed to connect Interstate 81 to Blacksburg.

### Day 10, June 2, Christiansburg to Fort Chiswell, VA, 52 miles

We hit the road very early, hoping to avoid the afternoon heat and humidity that had been getting progressively worse each day. The National Weather Service had also posted a hailstorm and flash flood warning for the evening.

A thick fog soon developed and we had to pull over and wait a half hour for it to lift. In Radford, we found a nice diner hidden down a back alley and enjoyed a late breakfast. At the two bike shops in town I inquired about a better rear-view mirror; on every steep downhill my helmet mounted one would feather in the wind. No luck. I was holding out for the wire-rimmed model that clipped onto one's glasses.

Today's countryside was a mix of run down farms and million dollar homes. Near Draper we were tipped off by the locals to refill our water bottles at an ice cold spring located nearby. The timing could have been better: I had just consumed a whole quart of chocolate milk.

Campgrounds with facilities seemed hard to find in this part of Virginia (Stephanie wasn't too broken up by this) so we stayed at a Super 8. Dinner consisted of cold Van Camps Beanie Weenie pork and beans. Yummy.

### Day 11, June 3, Fort Chiswell to Rural Retreat, VA, 24 miles

Today's ride took us through downtown Wytheville, home of famous "Skeeters" hotdogs (we had one for breakfast) and the world's biggest pencil (you can't miss it; it's mounted on the side of a building). We had a nice chat with Ron, a propane delivery man, who stopped to check on us as we were taking a nap off the side of the road. He envied our temporarily carefree and adventurous lifestyle, and insisted on giving us a twenty to help fund our upcoming lunch break.

After 24 miles we called it a day as the head winds were making our progress slow and painful. We found the hostel run by the Rural Retreat Historical Society, and soon the curator of the museum showed up and made us comfortable. Next on his agenda was a guided tour of the society's featured exhibit of Dr. Pepper.

"Dr. Charles Pepper was a Confederate surgeon during the Civil War, who later opened a drug store here in town," he related. "As the story goes, his pharmacist Charles Alderton fell in love with his daughter, but Dr. Pepper didn't approve of the romance. The heartbroken employee eventually left town and later settled in Waco, Texas, where he was employed at Morrison's Old Corner Drug Store. There he developed the fountain drink in 1885, one year before the introduction of Coca-Cola. Why he named it after Dr. Pepper, I'll never know."

Stephanie cooked up some pasta in the kitchen, one of the few times we prepared hot food on the entire trip. Later in the evening a very special cyclist joined us.

Allen was headed east, starting in St. Louis and ending in Washington, DC using a hand-pedaled bike for the disabled. He had recently lost the use of his legs from a rare disease that attacks one's nervous system. We stayed up until midnight talking, and he played his guitar and sang some songs that he wrote. His positive attitude and contagious sense of humor was inspirational. Through pledges of monetary support, Allen was raising funds and awareness for disabled athletes—many of whom were former servicemen—whom he eventually visited at Walter Reed Hospital when he arrived in Washington. Allen admitted to really missing his wife and two young daughters (who joined him in DC when he finished) and paid us a compliment by stating that we were the first people he'd met on his journey that he would have brought home for them to meet. We gladly donated Ron's twenty.

**Allan**

<u>Day 12, June 4, Rural Retreat to Damascus, VA, 47 miles</u>
<u>(519 miles total)</u>

We had a nice, shady ride through the Mt. Rogers National Forest today. A long but gentle climb took us to Troutdale, where we broke up the day with a leisurely lunch. On the way, we stopped to talk with a group of boy scouts who had just earned their backpacking badge on the AT and were waiting for a shuttle home.

There were lots of other people making use of this recreational area, including many horseback riders. We passed many outfitters' horse trailers parked at the trailheads. On the last downhill into Damascus, we paralleled the "Creeper Trail," a very popular rail trail for cyclists which has been a huge economic boom for the town. Damascus is also known as "the friendliest town on the Appalachian Trail" and its Trail Days every spring bring in thousands of enthusiastic hikers, including many AT alumni, who use the event as an opportunity to celebrate the backpacking way of life and to reconnect with friends they made while hiking the trail.

We stayed at The Place, a hostel run by the local church which is mostly used by hikers, although it was originally established for the BikeCentennial in 1976. We had about a half dozen thru hikers staying with us that night.

"BikeCentennial" was the brainchild of Greg Siple. The event (coordinated by the organization by the same name) was a mass ride of cyclists across the United States to celebrate the 200th anniversary of our country. Countless hours were put in by the staff to establish cycle camps in schools, churches, parks, and even homes along the route. They also trained several hundred leaders to escort the 4100 riders who would eventually participate (of which 2000 made it all the way). The organization would later evolve into the Adventure Cycling Association.

We managed to reach the Damascus post office before 5:00 PM, and picked up our mail drop—the first of several that we would receive from home during the course of our journey. It included a few surprises: chocolate and the local paper. In return we mailed back our unnecessary long john's (don't laugh—we would need them later) and a Mr. Potato Head toy for our grandson.

## Day 13, June 5, Damascus to Rosedale, VA, 34 miles

Before leaving Damascus, we enjoyed a hearty breakfast at Cowboys, famous for their blueberry pancakes. There we talked to "Cowboy" himself who gave us a brief history of Damascus.

"Twenty years ago the town had fallen into hard times, but then the Creeper Trail was built. Today Damascus is a lively community, with dozens of thriving businesses." When we got onto the subject of hikers on the Appalachian Trail, he had a confession to make. "I have a bad habit of hiding autographed rocks in hiker's backpacks. One day a group of pissed-off hikers, who had discovered the additional weight in their packs a few miles down the trail, returned to roll a 500 pound boulder in front of the entrance to my store, and no one could get in or out until I got a backhoe down here to move it."

By midday we had reached Hayters Gap, and we had a nice picnic lunch of tuna pre-mix and chips behind the library. Refueled, we began the grueling four mile climb up Clinch Mountain. Clinch Mountain, immortalized by the legendary Carter family in their 1928 song "My Clinch Mountain Home," was 150 miles wide, so there was no going around it.

After a quick descent down the other side, we arrived at the Elk Garden Methodist Church where we pitched the tent. We were unable to use the bathrooms or the kitchen, as by trial and error we discovered the sewer system was all backed up. Stephanie and I both took a very quick and refreshing outdoor shower under the garden hose before retiring!

## Day 14, June 6, Rosedale to Breaks Interstate Park, VA, 44 miles

We rose early again to beat the heat and enjoyed breakfast in Honaker at the Farmer's Kitchen. This "don't miss" diner was hiding behind the Chevrolet dealership and had the best home fries on our entire trip.

Good thing we had consumed all those carbohydrates, because Big A Mountain was next. We found out what the A stood for, as we cursed it as we ground our way up. Its long steep grades were deceivingly hidden by the winding climb. Later resting in Davenport, we replenished essential nutrients and electrolytes with ketchup flavored potato chips and by now our preferred recovery drink, chocolate milk.

By mid afternoon, a light drizzle slickened the twisty, hilly road. At the bottom of one of these hills we came upon an accident scene; a coal truck had jackknifed just minutes before we arrived. The driver, who was shaken but not hurt, claimed that he was forced to lock up his brakes by a motorist who had attempted a three point turn on the blind curve.

A few miles shy of Breaks Interstate Park the drizzle turned into a downpour. We continued on (now in full rain-gear) and when we finally turned up the park entrance I made the mistake of muttering something to the tune of "now let's find a nice campsite!"

"You've got to be kidding!" roared Stephanie, who detests camping in the rain. After her ensuing meltdown, featuring tears and profanity, I reconsidered and splurged on a room at the park's lodge. After taking a hot shower and slipping down in between a set of clean sheets on a soft mattress (that was just a wee bit thicker than a Thermarest), she was in much better spirits. Plus I knew that our planned day off tomorrow to take in the scenic park would put a smile on her face. To offset the cost of the room, we had a cold three-course meal of pita bread, beanie weenies, and corned beef.

## Day 15, June 7, Breaks Interstate Park, 0 miles

Not a great day off. Yesterday, when stopping to don our raingear, I had noticed the rear tire was rubbing on the chain stay (and that the chain was doing funky things). So in the morning, while Stephanie was off on what turned out to be major hike to find the laundry facilities, I began working on the bike. What I thought was simply an untrue wheel, which is easily fixed by adjusting a few spokes, turned out to be a broken cassette hub (not a common malady and hence we carried no spare). I went to the park office and with the help of the ladies at the desk we determined that the closest bike shop was back in Damascus. I gave it a call, and the mechanic believed he had a replacement for it on hand. And because I lacked the right sized allen wrench to install it, I decided the best course of action was for me to hitch-hike there with the broken wheel. By now it was 10 am, and I had a 160 mile round trip ahead of me. Not wanting to lose time tracking Stephanie down (we had only one cell phone between the two of us) I left her a note at the hotel room and hit the road.

I had never hitch-hiked in my life. My first lift was brief: a local guy out with his pickup cutting firewood. I was then picked up by an elderly couple, and judging by the way they bickered they had to have been married for 50 years. Upon telling them my desire to get to Damascus, Fred and Ethel informed me that they were headed in a slightly different direction, but because it was on a busier highway, I would stand a better chance of catching rides. I bought their logic and jumped in for what turned out to be a comical adventure. Their "busy road" theory was offset by the lost time incurred due to the many errands they had to make on the way. First stop was to pay their gas bill. Next was a hardware store where they had a lengthy discussion on what grit sandpaper they should buy. At McDonald's, Fred satisfied his daily McFlurry fix. While I joined him inside, I couldn't help but notice the commotion developing over at the neighboring filling station, where Ethel was going car to car, apparently quizzing everyone about the whereabouts of any nearby bike shops. I felt that I was living in a sitcom. Their last stop was at a convenient store to play their daily numbers, where I thanked them and began hitching again, still only half way to Damascus.

A few short rides later (from miners—this was coal country) I hopped in with Jim, a relatively young man. He was in the Navy, and having served on nuclear subs was now a recruiter. Although he was headed south to Tennessee, he was kind enough to drive out of his way and take me east to Damascus.

Finding the bike shop, I soon learned that the hub on hand was not the right fit; it was a special heavy duty one made just for tandem wheels. So much for the "heavy duty." By now it was after 5:00 PM, and we'd have to wait until morning to call around and get one coming. No sense staying in Damascus I thought, as it would take at least two days to arrive via UPS. Plus I was worried about Stephanie; I had left in a rush with only a brief note of my plans to hitchhike to Damascus. Bill the bike mechanic suggested I check with the outfitter next door, perhaps they had a van leaving to shuttle AT hikers to a trailhead which would be in my general direction.

I found "Crazy Horse" sitting outside the outfitters eating his dinner of cold ravioli out of a can. He wore a green New York Jets number 12 Joe Namath jersey nicely accented by pointy crocodile cowboy boots. The outfitter had personally fixed me up with him to shuttle me back to the "Breaks." During the 30 minutes it took him to fuel up his Toyota he began to tell me his life story. Among other things, he claimed to be a college graduate and to have thru-hiked the AT four times. I didn't recall much of the conversation during the drive; I was too preoccupied with prayer, as a goopy right eye impaired his vision and made him favor the center of the road. We arrived at the motel just before dark, where I paid Crazy Horse the agreed $100 for the 80 mile lift. Stephanie was very relieved to have me back in one piece.

## Day 16-17, June 8-9, Breaks Interstate Park, 0 miles

I got on the cell phone first thing in the morning and soon had a new hub coming from a tandem bike dealer, to be over-nighted directly to the bike shop in Damascus. We were hopeful that by the end of tomorrow our bike would be reassembled and Friday we could finally cross into Kentucky.

Stephanie suggested we inquire about a rental car, to simplify the logistics of going back to get our fixed wheel. Besides, we had two mail drops to pick up in the next couple days of riding, which looked like they would fall on the weekend. We could use the car to drive ahead for them, avoiding the possibility of losing more days waiting for the post office to re-open on Monday. It sounded like a brilliant plan to me.

After our rental was delivered, our first trip was to the other end of the park, relocating all of our gear to a campsite to save money. Soon after we were previewing our route into Kentucky, and we passed two westbound couples riding in the rain that day. The first we believe were Stephanie and Sebastian, but we couldn't stop to visit due to traffic. We had been reading all their entries in guest logs through Virginia, and would continue to read them across the US, but unfortunately would never meet them. We stopped and chatted with a second couple (from Colorado), oblivious to the pouring rain, anxious to get to Bardstown in a few days to enjoy the "Bourbon Capital of the World!" At the Hindman post office we picked up the first of our mail drops: some maps and supplies, and later in Booneville, our second: some homemade Christata (an Italian pastry) from my brother Steve and wife Amy.

The next day the cold front lifted and we took a tour of the Breaks Interstate Park, driving along the park road and stopping at all the scenic overlooks. The gorge was carved by the Russell Fork River over thousands of years. Down at the bottom of the gorge, railroad tracks parallel the river, and freight trains haul thousands of tons of coal through the gorge and its tunnels every day.

## Day 18, June 10, Breaks Interstate Park, 0 miles

We were beginning to go stir crazy at the Breaks, and with our part due to arrive today, we left early in the morning with the rental car for Damascus. In Honaker we passed a supported group of cyclists riding for Multiple Sclerosis. We would bump into them again in a few days (this time on our bike) and get to talk.

Once in Damascus, we set up our stake-out, parking across the street from the bike shop, trying to look inconspicuous. Sure enough, around late morning a brown, marked van showed up and with a little old driver so lively and quick, we knew in a moment it must be our part! And when that little package appeared in his hand, we felt like kids on Christmas morning! We ran inside to verify that it in fact was our cassette hub, where Bill the mechanic gave us the good and the bad news. The good—that it was indeed our part, and the bad—that the reassembly would have to wait a while.

"I'll be back in an hour," he announced while heading for the back door. "My mom's in town, and she's 83 today. I'm taking her to lunch not only because it's her birthday, but because I'm still feeling guilty about having to take away the keys to her motorcycle." When he returned he installed the new cassette hub and we were back in business. On the way "home" to the Breaks, we stopped in Lebanon and celebrated by dining at the Bonanza steak house.

# CHAPTER 3

## KENTUCKY

### *Humid, Hot, and Hilly*

<u>Day 19, June 11, Breaks Interstate Park to Hindman, KY, 70 miles</u>
We resumed cycling the next day after returning the rental car. During the three mile downhill into Elkhorn City we passed the state line. A coal truck caught up to us on the bridge over the Russell Fork River, and although there was a car coming in the opposite direction, he decided he needed to pass us right there and then (rumor has it they get paid by the load—not by the hour). With no shoulder on the two lane bridge, I riveted my attention to the white line and kept the front wheel glued to it as the truck passed within inches of us!

Today turned out to be one of the toughest days of our entire trip. It included three unrelenting, winding hill climbs totaling almost 4000 feet, under very hot and humid conditions. Near Virgie we caught up to a chatted with a handful of the MS riders, all college-aged kids. In Bevinsville, we had to pull up as I was disabled by a nasty cramp in my calf. A kind gentleman next door came out with several ice-cold bottles of water, which we thanked him for and promptly mixed with our powdered Gatorade, figuring it would help the cramp from returning. It did the trick, and we made it over the last big hill. Then around 6 PM near Pippa Passes, a nasty thunderstorm blew up, and we took refuge (with permission) on a front porch. The homeowner was down on his luck, recently laid off as a result of a coal mine closure. "Coal is King" around here, and if its use is phased out, the region's economy would go from bad to worse.

The skies cleared an hour later, and we calculated we had just enough daylight to make it to Hindman and the Knott County Historical Society's B & B, where we had made reservations. It was a cyclist's heaven on earth, despite the thirty percent grade quarter-mile long driveway. Dave, our gracious host, met us at the top (a motion detector tipped him off of our arrival) with tall glasses of ice tea. After calling in our pizza order (to be delivered), we showered while Dave did our laundry and fixed us two of his renowned baked sweet potatoes, drizzled with pure maple syrup and topped with a generous dollop of whipped cream. Did we forget to mention the ice cream sundaes that followed? After some great conversation by the campfire, we passed out on the pre-inflated one-foot thick air mattresses in his pre-erected circus tent.

Dave had his share of animals; at least a dozen cats roamed the place. The B & B was also a turtle "refuge." People brought him box turtles; he estimated there were over 100 on the grounds. It was their breeding season, and Dave had witnessed six different positions. He swore he detected a smile on the face of one of the males after a particular mating, as the turtle laid on his back for hours afterwards. Dave thought mankind could learn a lot from them and their slow-paced lifestyle (as they live to the ripe old age of 100).

## Day 20, June 12, Hindman to Booneville, KY, 63 miles

The morning broke with a light drizzle, so we rolled over in our sleeping bags and slept in until 9 AM. After a breakfast of strawberry shortcake and fruit, we talked with Dave while it continued to sprinkle off and on. Just before noon we rolled out of town, the weather again hazy, hot and humid. During the day we managed to dodge three thunderstorms that all went around us. After climbing a prolonged grade by Buckhorn Lake, we arrived in Booneville just before dusk to pick up some groceries for dinner and breakfast. At the supermarket we met a couple of the MS riders; they had camped on a church lawn in town. We had reservations for the cottage at Linda's Victorian Rose B and B, a nicer alternative than trying to get a good night's sleep in a hot tent.

**Love those down hills! A well-earned one near Buckhorn, Kentucky**

## Day 21, June 13, Booneville to Berea, KY, 48 miles

I had a hard time getting Stephanie out of bed the next morning, and after I served her breakfast in bed I began looking for the cattle prod. She finally got up after I threatened to turn off the air conditioner.

Upon previewing today's route on our maps, we noticed that the road would take us up and over the "Big Hill" (and into the town of the same name), and with a moniker like that it didn't take a rocket scientist to figure it could be trouble. However, after climbing up a not-so-big hill (which turned out to be the one and only "Big Hill"), we found ourselves looking down the other side where the road went through the mother of all rock cuts. All that worry over nothing.

As we pulled into the Super 8 in Berea at the end of another long, hot, hilly day, there it was—the POOL. In an instant the buckles on our bulging panniers were unsnapped and their contents thrown across the room in a search for our swim suits! After the refreshing plunge, we bobbed around in the deep end—too tired to actually swim.

During the first few weeks of our trip, I was constantly assessing every piece of gear: had we used it yet? If not would we need it? Could we improvise without it? I had been using a bag of clothes as a pillow, and I admit it was a little lumpy. Stephanie had the Cadillac of camping pillows, a "Thermarest," which I kept threatening to ship back home. Now that we had the worst days in the Appalachians behind us, I gave in. In fact, if you can't beat 'em, join 'em! At a gift shop in Berea I bought my own discount pillow for five dollars.

## Day 22, June 14, Berea to Harrodsburg, KY, 43 miles

We had a little scare today. While pushing the bike up an especially steep grade, I looked back at Stephanie and noticed a big glob of blood on her leg! We cleaned it up but couldn't find any cut. Looking back downhill a few feet, we solved the mystery, a rolled-over ketchup packet flattened on the pavement.

We managed to dodge two more thunderstorms today including the one that blew around us at midnight while we were snug in our tent at Chimney Rock campground. Our sister-in-law Lynn, who is a professor of Meteorology at the University of Washington, was serving as our own personal Emergency Broadcast System during the trip (via email), and in the event of an actually emergency we would have been instructed to seek shelter. It was reassuring to see her emails each day, warning us of upcoming "cells" and "inversion events" (although it was unlikely we were about to outrun them on a bike).

At the campground we discovered that Kentucky is infected with an invasive, noxious species. It grows to be about three feet tall in only five years. Its name is Eugene and he's the spitting image of Sid, the devilish kid next door in the movie *Toy Story*. He was actually trying to fly his "Buzz Light Year" toy into the pavement during our stay. Although we announced that we were retiring to our tent to "sleep" (well before sundown), Sid managed a couple more laps around our tent in his motorized razor scooter.

### Day 23, June 15, Harrodsburg to Bardstown, KY, 54 miles

We awoke bright and early, determined to sneak out of camp before Eugene woke up. To celebrate that accomplishment, we enjoyed a hearty breakfast at The Bus Station in Harrodsburg. By now a leisurely breakfast at a hometown diner had become one of the highlights of each day. Besides, Stephanie got cranky if she didn't get her daily half-pound ration of bacon. I had developed a weakness for the bottomless cup of joe and biscuits smothered in sausage gravy with a side of home-fries. Many cyclists crave pancakes, but a short-stack never seemed to appeal to us. Now that we had a few weeks of cycling behind us (including some "beyond category" climbs in the Appalachians) we had discovered what were to become the Four Building Blocks of our nutritional requirements: bacon, eggs, ketchup, and chocolate milk—lots of chocolate milk. Sort of like the food pyramid in the shape of Mesa Verde.

The hills eased up today, although the heat and humidity stayed with us. We toured the Lincoln Homestead State Park where Abe's parents first lived. In Bardstown (home of Stephen Foster) we made camp at My Old Kentucky Home campground. We tried to take a nap before dinner but it was stifling in the tent. We killed some time at the Laundromat, drinking lukewarm beer out of brown paper bags while severe tornado warnings for southern Indiana (just to the north of us) were being flashed across a television. Later that night we did survive a thunderstorm which rolled through.

## Day 24, June 16, Bardstown to Hodgenville, KY, 42 miles

Allen, the hand-cyclist, had recommended a detour to the Abbey of Our Lady of Gethsemane, which is home to a society of monks. While there we bought a block of their limburger cheese at the gift shop, but couldn't stomach eating more than half of it. Luckily, the gift shop also stocked the fruit preserves of their Brothers from Spencer, Massachusetts who make a delicious strawberry-rhubarb jam which was more than adequate to cleanse the palate.

The rolling hills, covered with crops of tobacco, beans and corn, had brought us to Kentucky's "Land of Lincoln." We stopped at Lincoln's birthplace but passed on his boyhood home—which we deemed too far off route.

## Day 25, June 17, Hodgenville to Falls of Rough, KY, 62 miles

We enjoyed another great breakfast, this time at Brooks Cafe in Sonora, Kentucky. Shortly after we arrived, three wise men wandered in from afar for the meatloaf special. Roger and his buddies proved to be very friendly and entertaining as they quizzed us about our travels thus far.

That night we found ourselves at the Rough River Dam, in the Central Time Zone, where we camped for the night. There we met a family cycling from Seattle. Keith and his college-aged son and daughter were headed east, putting in long hours on the saddle to cover the last thousand miles, as they were running low on funds.

We were awakened in the middle of the night by a crunching sound. A raccoon had managed to unzip our food bag and make off with our bagels and potato chips. Back to hanging the food.

## Day 26, June 18, Falls of Rough to Owensboro, KY, 45 miles (1,024 miles total)

At Fiddler's restaurant after bacon and eggs, Stephanie insisted I take a picture of her next to the life-size cardboard figures of James Dean and his green grandmother.

Today was full of milestones and firsts: our odometer went over 1000 miles, I had two chocolate shakes within one hour (it was so hot the chocolate milk wasn't potent enough), and we experienced our first flat tire (which I was changing in record time until Ralphie spilled all the lug nuts). We also ate frog's legs for the first time in our lives (an unlabeled mystery—we thought they were mutant chicken drumsticks); they were featured at the Shoney's Friday night fried fish buffet. And they did taste like chicken.

### Day 27, June 19, Owensboro to Sebree, KY, 36 miles

It was a short, relatively flat day. We passed acres and acres of corn, soybeans and wheat, most of which we assumed would be consumed by the millions of chickens and turkeys that inhabit the many poultry barns in the area.

It was sunny and hot again but at least today there was a breeze. The hot spell we've encountered had forced us to develop a strategic plan to cope with these conditions. First on the list was shade management. On long uphill grinds, an oasis of shade was chosen at regular intervals where we would rest, rehydrate, and rain sweat. Secondly, we had noticed that about 50% of the towns in Kentucky had a dollar store. We had taken advantage of this situation to the upmost. Every store in this particular chain was cooled by air conditioning to the approximate temperature of the Siberian tundra. Must be the owners emigrated from Russia (across the land bridge to save money—everyone knows that Titanic tickets cost more than a dollar) and kept the stores at this temperature to remind them of the old country. Anyway, Stephanie would stroll up and down the aisles until her beads of sweat froze up. Meanwhile, I would test out the durability of the plastic patio furniture on display (i.e. sit and rest on it). After about a half hour, Stephanie would finally check out with a gallon of water and a bag of ice.

During a rest break near Utica, we met Vic, a retired truck driver who inquired about our route. When we told him we were headed out west, it triggered this memory of his from Montana:

> "I had a job driving a rig in the western part of the state, with a route short enough so that I could make two round trips each day. Then one day, I decided to stop at a trout stream and try my luck. I hooked lots of fish and decided that wetting a few lines there would become part of my daily routine, even though my doing so would limit me to one round trip."

"After a while, my boss discovered this drop in my productivity, so he secretly followed me one day to see what was going on. He caught me fishing, and came down to the bank to tell me that when I got back to the warehouse to stop in the office to pick up my last paycheck. I told him fair enough, but since you're here and I have an extra rod in the truck we might as well make the best of it and continue fishing."

"We both spent the rest of the afternoon fishing together, catching lots of fish. Upon leaving, my boss informed me that he couldn't remember the last time he had such an enjoyable, peaceful afternoon, and to just ignore that comment about picking up my last paycheck. I continued to make just one round trip a day, and my boss never said another word about it."

We pedaled into Sebree by early afternoon, and found our great accommodations at the First Baptist Church (the town boasts 10 different churches in a town of only 1500 people) where we had access to a shower, laundry facilities, mattresses, air-conditioning, and a refrigerator which was stocked with all the chocolate milk we could drink! And the best was yet to come: when we quizzed Bob the pastor about the best place to dine in town, he proudly replied, "my wife Violet's kitchen! She loves to cook for visiting cyclists." He also tipped us off on some pre-dinner entertainment down at a local establishment known as the "Purple Opry," which featured senior citizen karaoke with back up from the local musicians.

Later we returned to Bob and Violet's, where we were treated to a delicious home-cooked meal and an evening of great conversation, fellowship, and prayer.

# CHAPTER 4

## ILLINOIS

*Pirates, Pizza, and Popeye*

### Day 28, June 20, Sebree, KY to Cave in Rock, IL 57 miles

We received phone calls from all of our kids today, wishing me a happy Father's Day. Our ride took us through some pleasant farm country with easy rolling hills. We arrived just in time at the dock on the Ohio River to board the small boat that would ferry us to the other side of the muddy river and into Illinois. Unfortunately a few river tugs pushing humongous barges had the right-of-way, so we had to wait at the dock for an extra half hour, choking on the exhaust of the idling cars (running their AC units) that we shared the ferry with. After finally reaching the other side, a short ride took us to a campground at Cave in Rock State Park. The park's namesake overlooks the Ohio, and it was used by pirates as a hide out after raiding riverboats back in the days of the sternwheelers.

Now four weeks into our ride, we had managed to start some pretty good cyclist tans. Being a dairy farmer for many years, I had been envied for my sexy "farmer tan" (just look for the guy in the pool with brown arms but otherwise as white as a ghost). We had graduated from that version to the classic cyclist tan, featuring the addition of bronzed legs but with the tell-tale white hands and feet. My receding hairline made it possible for me to also display the stripes of a "helmet vent Mohawk" on my scalp.

Speaking of tans, we had managed to baffle cyclists we'd met by being able to guess with uncanny accuracy the direction of which they were doing the TransAm route. Our secret: the orientation of their tan. Darker on the left means going west. Darker on the right—headed east. An even tan means they're riding north-south, they've gotten lost too many times or they're just faking the trip by stopping at a tanning bed now and then. Another giveaway was if they passed us from behind or from the front.

## Day 29, June 21, Cave in Rock to Vienna, IL, 51 miles

Another scorcher. We were out of the campground by 7:00 AM to beat the heat (although it never really cooled off much during the night). We rolled along the Ohio River to Golconda, where we rehydrated with chocolate milk. The owner was kind enough to supply free ice to refill our water bottles (people everywhere had been so generous with the ice) and we headed back out in the heat. We passed a beautiful cypress swamp and some tidy Amish farms. After a rest stop at a chocolate factory where we sampled (you guessed it) chocolate, Stephanie and I opted for the cooler treat, ice cream. It was a relatively short finish into Vienna where we quickly found a motel with a POOL!

Once settled into our motel, a craving for pizza and beer overtook us (our diet had been dangerously deficient in these important foodstuffs due to the many "dry" counties in Kentucky). I inquired at the front desk whether there was a pizza place in town that delivered. An employee informed me that "Casey's" ("just a little ways up the street") made pizza but did not deliver. Obtaining their phone number, I ordered one and began walking (after a long day in the saddle and a cool refreshing dip in the pool, getting back on the bike was NOT an option). In the meantime Stephanie volunteered to walk across the street to a convenient store to get the beer.

In 1000 feet I passed an open restaurant sporting the following sign on their roof: "Newt's Pizza—We deliver." What the heck? But I figured this Casey's place couldn't be that much further, so I continued on. One and a half miles later, I arrived at Casey's, a glorified gas station, to pick up my pizza. Upon my return to the motel a long hour later, a worried Stephanie met me at the door. I threw the pizza on the bed and exclaimed, "Oh, you weren't expecting this tonight we're you?"

It wasn't the first time we'd met someone clueless about their hometown, although some people could give us detailed directions to a Wal-Mart 40 miles away that could rival MapQuest's. Maybe if more people took an interest in their own community, hometown USA would be a little better off.

## Day 30, June 22, Vienna to Carbondale, IL, 43 miles

Our early-bird strategy was of no advantage today. As we rode past the Vienna bank at 7:00 AM its sign posted the temperature at 86 degrees. Fortunately, it was a short day mileage wise and not too hilly. The highlight was the ride through Crab Orchard Wildlife Refuge and past Devil's Kitchen Lake on a quiet, shady country road. There was a cool breeze blowing off the lake, its rippling waves sparkling in the sun. We found along its shores a shady oak tree where we enjoyed a picnic lunch.

We arrived in the college town of Carbondale shortly after noon, where our first stop was at the bike shop to get a stubborn pedal squeak taken care of (turned out it was coming from my shoe) and to pick up a new helmet with a sun visor for Stephanie. There Julie (a reporter from the local newspaper) intercepted us, took a few pictures, and quizzed us on our trip.

After checking into the Super 8, we split up to do errands. While Stephanie went to get her hair cut short to better deal with the heat (pictures of her Dorothy Hamill "bob" were to draw many accolades to our blog), my first mission was to pick up a mail drop at the post office.

The post office in Carbondale was so large that I had to take a number. When I finally got to the counter, the clerk, after searching for ten minutes, could not locate a "general delivery" package with our name on it. I stepped outside, and called my son-in-law Ken on our phone. He assured me that about a week ago he mailed out the next set of maps (as requested) in a brown envelope. So I went back inside, took another number, and waited in line to double check. This time I was waited on by a different clerk, so after filling him in on my missing parcel, I asked him if there was any chance it would still arrive after a week.

"It should have been here by now," was his response.

"So you're saying it's lost?" I replied.

"Oh we don't like to use that word here at the post office," he countered.

Just about then I spotted a lone brown envelope behind him on a shelf. Pointing to it I asked, "Could that be it?"

Walking back and picking it up he read, "General Delivery for Michael Battisti?"

My next errand was to the Laundromat, which, according to the motel staff, was "only a quarter of a mile away." After the mile-plus trek to it, I was convinced that since the invention of the automobile the general public has lost all sense of distance.

### Day 31, June 23, Carbondale to Chester, IL, 50 miles

Today we caught up to the Heinle's. We had been hearing rumors of a family of five traveling by bicycle (using two tandems and a single bike) just a day or two ahead of us. After rehydrating in Ava, we spotted some cyclists ahead, and as we gained on them we could see that sure enough it included two tandems—the traveling Heinle family! Of all the days to meet them, today we were on a tight schedule. Stephanie, being a member of Rotary (the community service organization), was hell-bent on making it to Chester in time to attend their weekly meeting at noon. She carried a notepad with all the towns we were to travel through across America which had a Rotary club, and the time and day of the week on which they met. Until today, our itinerary had not coincided with any club meetings. Now as we finally had the Heinle's in our sights, she warned me as we approached, "There's no time to socialize!"

We did introduced ourselves as we passed and asked them where we could chat with them that night, and they informed us they would staying at the Best Western. We then speed off and made the meeting with just minutes to spare. From then on, whenever I needed more help from my stoker, I simply yelled, "Better put on those Rotary legs!"

Later that afternoon we visited with the Heinle's. Originally traveling self-supported, Denny, his son and three daughters were relieved that Mom had just arrived with the family car to provide SAG for the rest of the trip (they would also end in Seattle but by a different route). They admitted that the steep grades of the eastern hills had taken a toll on them, and that after crossing the Mississippi tomorrow they were planning to detour north to pick up the "Katy Trail," thereby avoiding the Ozark Mountains of Missouri. The Katy Trail, at 225 miles, is the longest Rails-to-Trails project in the United States. It runs west from St. Louis along the old railroad bed of the Missouri-Kansas and Texas Railroad.

Denny's wife Kitty suggested that we take their car for a trip downtown for dinner that night, which we did. A wonderful act of kindness towards total strangers!

**The Heinle's**

# CHAPTER 5

# MISSOURI

*Refreshing Rivers*

<u>Day 32, June 24, Chester, IL to Farmington, Missouri, 48 miles</u>

As we left Chester, Stephanie took a few pictures of the many Popeye statues around town. Elzie Segar, the creator of the famous comic strip, was born here and the characters he drew were based on actual inhabitants he knew in Chester.

Under high cloud cover and relatively cool temperatures for a change, we headed over the swollen Mississippi. We knew the bridge was long, had only two lanes and no shoulder. But we were there by 7:00 AM so the traffic was very light. The bridge went over Horse Island, an encampment of Lewis and Clark early in their epic journey. The next 10 miles were glorious—the Mississippi floodplain on the Missouri side was very flat, and with an unexpected tailwind from the east we were given a rare opportunity to use our big chainring!

Unfortunately, those conditions ended as we approached St. Mary, where a series of roller coaster hills began. While fueling up on our chocolate milk at a little store, we had a nice chat with the locals about the summer's crops. Almost all the dairy farms had gone out in favor of large corn, soybean and wheat farms. They also told us how close to them the Mississippi's waters had reached during the big flood of '93—and how they hoped it never happened again. Just the thought of handling all those sandbags gave them a backache!

After getting bored of the same variety of road kill for 1300 miles (usually snakes, squirrels, box turtles, and the occasional possum), we we're excited to see some fresh armadillo in Missouri!

We rolled into Farmington around 1:00 PM and had no trouble finding Al's Place, the local bike hostel founded in memory of a local businessman (and avid cyclist) who was extremely active in the community but sadly lost his fight with cancer.

Farmington also has a vibrant "old downtown," and we spent several hours making stops at:

1. the coffee shop, for a latte
2. the barbershop, where I got my hair buzzed very short. Shortest it's been since I was born
3. the post office, to mail out used maps, souvenirs, and miscellaneous unwanted ballast
4. the local health food store, where the owner Marylee told us to make sure we stopped to see her son, a park ranger at Grand Teton National Park, and to tell him she said hello!
5. The Factory, which is in fact an old factory, converted into a fantastic gallery of little shops, booths, and restaurants
6. The Firehouse Pub and Grill, where we dined on fried green beans, sweet potato fries with melted marshmallow dipping sauce, and sandwiches. We passed on the deep-fried pickles, and couldn't find room for the fried Oreos for dessert. We were willing to endanger our blood pressure and cholesterol levels to sample the ethnic foods the area had to offer.

## Day 33, June 25, Farmington to Centerville, MO, 48 miles

We were on the road before 6:00 AM under partly sunny skies, with temperatures almost cool enough to need our arm warmers. The first 16 miles went fast, and we were recharging with chocolate milk in Pilot Knob before we knew it. And when we began to climb the foothills of the Ozarks, the wind shifted around from the east and kept pushing us along at a good clip. Approaching the Ozarks, we entered a mix of conifer and hardwood forest, and the warming morning sun produced the sweet fragrance of melting pitch from those pines.

By midmorning we had arrived at Johnson's Shut-Ins State Park. During summer vacations, this place attracts hot, bored kids like honey attracts bees. Here the East Fork of the Black River flows through a volcanic ryolite formation, and had cut and sculpted enough chutes, bowls, and little water falls so that every kid (and parent) had his own little water park. We cooled off in a few holes before eating a picnic lunch. It was a great way to break up the day.

**Cooling off at Johnson's Shut-Ins State Park**

Back in 2005 the earthen dam of a reservoir on top of nearby Proffit Mountain broke loose and a wall of water swept tons of boulders, trees, and earth down into the park. Luckily it was in December and no one was around. A new visitor's center tells all about the catastrophic event and the extensive restoration project that followed.

Back on the road, we encountered some short steep grades the last thirteen miles into Centerville, a cute little village featuring great food at The 21 Diner. With the cool, crystal clear waters of the West Fork of the Black River for our bathing pleasure and the county courthouse providing its lawn for our campsite, we were all set for the night.

## Day 34, June 26, Centerville to Eminence, MO, 45 miles

Today we entered the Ozark Mountains and started climbing some significant hills. There we met our second east-bound through cyclist, carrying a full sized floor pump among other things. He wasn't very talkative.

A much needed rest break at a cemetery was cut short due to some pesky black flies, so we pretty much high-tailed it into Eminence, a Mecca for rafters floating the Jack's Fork River. Depressed that we had arrived too late in the afternoon to rent a tube and catch a shuttle up river, we underwent ice cream therapy at the Frosty Freeze and later had a dosage of air-conditioning and a soft bed at The Pines Crest Cabins.

## Day 35, June 27, Eminence to Houston, MO, 44 miles

Today's mantra was "One less hill to Kansas." As we rolled out of Eminence this morning it was so humid the roads were sweating. After six miles we stopped at Alley Spring, which pumps out over 80 million gallons of turquoise-hued water a day. It was once used to power a turbine, which is still on display at a mill nearby. There are hundreds of springs in the Ozarks responsible for the cool, clear rivers we've been bathing in.

The climbing continued into Summersville where a stiff headwind developed and battled us as we followed a ridge the rest of the way into Houston. We met another east-bounder today, Eddie from Colorado. He was supported by his wife Bobbie, driving close behind in a pickup camper. We looked forward to these encounters getting more frequent as the days progressed.

### Day 36, June 28, Houston to Marshfield, MO, 66 miles

Much less heat and humidity made for a much more enjoyable day. The rolling hills continued through beef and horse ranches. A few Amish farmers were out toiling in their fields, harvesting wheat with antique horse-drawn reaper/binders.

We also met two college-aged brothers from Sweden who were traveling east. They had lots of questions for us about dogs, coal trucks and hills. We couldn't help notice that they were both all dressed in black, and Stephanie highly recommended that they at least attach a slow moving vehicle (SMV) triangle to the back of their bikes to make themselves more visible to traffic. We in fact used the orange "pennant-on-a-stick" for the duration of our trip (only taking it down on the windiest of days to reduce resistance).

Tonight we camped in the Marshfield city park, complete with an Olympic-sized swimming pool, bathroom, showers and very loud insects buzzing in the trees. Despite our earplugs, Stephanie had a miserable night's sleep, as she was bothered by a mild case of poison ivy from going in the bushes.

### Day 37, June 29, Marshfield to Everton, MO, 58 mi. (1571 total)

The first half of the day we flew over gently rolling farmland aided by a nice tailwind. Stephanie coined this terrain "ribbon candy hills." By late morning more significant hills had appeared. We stopped in Walnut Grove at a nice diner for a burger and pie. The diner was filled with construction workers, busy putting in a new town sewer system to re-enact the lost episode of *Little House on the Prairie.* Remember? The one where Laura finds the gold nugget down by the creek and she wants to trade it for some orthodontic work on her overbite so Alonzo will ask her to the harvest dance? Anyway, at the last minute she comes to her senses and gives it to Pa who uses it to fund the public works sewage project, bringing economic stimulus to the fair city of Walnut Grove.

After several more hills, we pulled into Everton, proud home of the Shaven Beaver Bar and Grill. There we were informed that we had unfortunately missed the popular Jell-O wrestling matches by a few days.

Just out of town we checked into our accommodations for the night, the plush Running Spring Farm, a pheasant hunting preserve with a beautiful rustic lodge, which made my old hunting shack look like a dive.

# CHAPTER 6

## KANSAS

*Prairie Pedaling*

The Top Ten Reasons Not to Bike Thru Kansas on a Cross-Country Trip:

1. least number of Elvis sightings in the lower 48
2. State bird is the flying monkey
3. Petrified Toto droppings every mile or so
4. A porous southern border which doesn't keep out Texans who barrel into Oklahoma to spy on the Okies and end up tumbling right into Kansas
5. Civil unrest due to the lingering Lollipop Guild strike
6. Maryanne still hasn't returned from the Island
7. First 1/4 of Kansas is all in black and white
8. Incessant "OOO-EEE-OOO" chanting rides the wind
9. Wheat, wheat, wheat, wheat, bump, wheat, wheat, wheat, wheat, bump
10. TWISTER!!!

Stay safe,
Chris
(blog comment)

## Day 38, June 30, Everton, MO to Pittsburg, Kansas, 65 miles

We immediately loved Kansas. It was flat. And Stephanie couldn't wait for me to drag her through all the barb-wire museums on the prairie.

The Kansas highway signs supposedly have a yellow sunflower around the route number (The state's nickname is the "Sunflower State"—but we hadn't seen any yet). But upon careful inspection of a sign, we determined it was actually a large 52-tooth golden chainring, reminding the touring cyclist that yes, you do have one down there on your crankset and in this state you could actually use it!

But first we had the last of the Ozark roller coaster hills to polish off. We hit the road with perhaps the coolest temperatures of our trip, and after about 15 miles Lynn's (our weather consultant's) promised tailwind from the east arrived! It felt like Stephanie had raised the mizzen mast up behind us! We flew into Golden City, *Missouri* for a late breakfast at Cookie's Diner, where we wished we had left room for a piece of their extensive selection of home-made pie.

Back on the road, the countryside turned into a checkerboard of corn, soybean, and wheat fields, diced up by roads at right angles at every mile. The tailwind continued, and in no time (by high-noon) we arrived in Pittsburg—our shortest day time wise by far. The American flag was whipping steadily westward as we pulled in to the Lamplighter Inn (our highly self-rated accommodations—i.e. pool). We were tempted to push on further —but we needed our rest. Tomorrow was another day, and Lynn reassured us that the tailwind would be there for a couple more days to push us westward.

The one thing lacking at the Lamplighter was laundry facilities, so Stephanie snuck over to the Holiday Inn Express across the street and did our laundry there. Cyclists have been "stealth" camping on the trail for years, but let it be known that we were the first to commit "stealth laundering".

## Day 39, July 1, Pittsburg to Chanute, KS, 62 miles

We feasted on the world's best continental breakfast at the Lamplighter Inn before leaving Pittsburg. The flag was still blowing in our favorable direction as we headed out of town under sunny skies and ideal temperatures. And to top it off, here in the plains the humidity had dropped considerably.

In Girard, we stopped at the post office to pick up a care package our son Zachary had sent us: Gatorade powder, butt butter, toiletries, and a new set of chains (remember, a tandem has two). Upon showing the postmaster my identification, he handed me one of those white plastic USPS totes, explaining nonchalantly, "There was some red powder leaking out of box [the Gatorade]. So we just threw the whole thing in here until you showed up. No big deal." I guess the big anthrax scare was officially over.

We arrived in Chanute early in the afternoon. The city was named after Octave Chanute, a brilliant railroad and bridge-building engineer, who later in life worked on the development of gliders and collaborated with the Wright Brothers. The town was also a stop on the Santa Fe Trail.

While updating our blog in the city library, a gentleman about our age in cycling attire approached me, and introduced himself as Gill.

"I couldn't help but notice your bike outside," he said.

I logged off, and we took the conversation outside.

"Back in '76 all of my friends tried to get me to go on the BikeCentennial Ride with them. But I couldn't get away. I've been regretting it ever since. Then last winter I lost my job, so here I am!" Gill was traveling fully loaded, but only covering a modest 30 miles a day. It occurred to us that at that rate he would be forced to trade his bike in for a pair of skis upon reaching the Rockies.

We joined Gill for a cold beer and some pleasant conversation in his motel room, and looked forward to seeing him on the road tomorrow. We soon found our accommodations, the city park, where we set up camp, changed the bike's chains, and then took in some sandlot baseball under the lights.

### Day 40, July 2, Chanute to Eureka, KS, 66 miles

We pedaled out of Chanute after eating breakfast at The Grain Bin, the morning hotspot. We had learned that if we just ride up and down a few city blocks at 7:00 AM each morning and locate the densest cluster of parked pickup trucks, we've found the best place for breakfast.

By mid-morning we rolled into downtown Toronto, population 312, where the banner stretched across Main Street proclaimed that the annual "Toronto Days" were to officially start tomorrow. We spotted Gill resting in the shade of the storefronts. "My sister called, and apparently I've bounced a few checks," he informed us.

"I'll straighten it out with this internet banking thing. Unfortunately, I have a little time to kill; the library doesn't open for two hours."

No sooner had we pulled over, when on cue from across the street came Jean Marie from the Senior Citizen's Center. "Why don't you all come on over and mingle with the VIP's of Chanute? We've got coffee and iced tea!" she announced.

The morning coffee social was just adjourning, but not before we answered lots of questions about our travels. We also got a complete rundown of the program of events on the eve of Toronto Days, including the parade, which Jean Marie estimated would take all of four minutes. Between that and the thought of missing the Big Breakfast, the Burger Feed, the Ice cream social, the Mud tug-of-war, and the Mud Races (not to mention the fireworks) we had a hard time getting back on the road to finish the ride to Eureka. For Gill however, the events were too hard to resist. Besides, Jean Marie had invited him over to use her internet, eliminating his wait at the library. He decided to stick around, maybe for a few days or possibly the rest of his life.

We reconnected via email with Gil almost a year later. Boy, had we underestimated him. On December 23rd near Phoenix, Arizona he wrote:

> I had duct tape on the tires and funny bulges from running over some steel on I-10 so I had my Forest Gump, "I think I'll stop now moment" at a bike shop and did stop after 6200 miles.

Just before Eureka, we entered the "Flint Hills," one of the biggest cattle grazing areas on the plains, where native grasses finish the cattle before they head to the stockyards. We had no issues with these "hills."

After the "Healthy Combo" meal (chocolate shake and a salad) at the Sonic Drive-In (no luck hanging our tray on the bike), we checked in at the adequate Bluestem Motel, yes, pool included.

**The Sonic Drive-In**

## Day 41, July 3, Eureka to Newton, KS, 74 miles

On our way out of Eureka, we bumped into five other east-bound cyclists, two of whom we had the pleasure of conversing with during breakfast at the Copper Kettle. The young men were unfortunately running out of time and money, and were detouring to Chicago to curtail their trip.

We could see bands of rain showers in all directions as we headed west into a stiff crosswind. Luckily, our route turned north after 19 miles and we were flying with a tailwind for the next 17 mile leg to Cassoday, the "Prairie Chicken Capital of the World."

Our route then swung due west again, for 38 incredibly straight miles. We rode through Mennonite country and recently harvested fields of their Turkey Red wheat, a variety that they brought with them when they emigrated from the Ukraine.

Our luck ran out about 25 miles shy of Newton, when a steady band of showers finally caught up to us. We pulled on our raincoats and continued on to our accommodations in Newton, the Econolodge, where we decided to celebrate the Fourth of July with our first rest day in over three weeks.

## Day 42, Independence Day, Newton, KS, 0 miles

We chose wisely; while holed up in Newton it rained steadily for 36 hours. Life was good here at the Econolodge. We did laundry, dried out our gear, and cleaned and lubed the bike chains. On a more relaxing note, we wrote postcards in bed while enjoying the All-American John Wayne Weekend on a Japanese flat-screen TV in a hotel room in the Heartland of America. Is there not a more patriotic way to spend Independence Day?

## Day 43, July 5, Newton to Nickerson, KS, 56 miles

We took advantage of the 11:00 AM check out time at the motel to hopefully wait out the last of the steady showers. We took to the road under gloomy conditions, but with our secret weapon: our deluxe Wal-Mart shopping bag shoe covers. As soon as we reached the other side of Newton, buckets started to fall from the sky and the only thing that kept our spirits up was the thought of a hot cup of Joe and supposedly the best donuts west of the Mississippi in Hesston (we had actually skimped on the continental breakfast because of this recommended stop). Our hearts sank when we saw the closed sign outside Daylite Donuts, and we had to settle for sustenance at a Subway. Being somewhat damp, we almost developed hypothermia inside the store due to the fact that they had the air conditioner cranked to the "Valley Forge" setting. Stephanie and I actually used the electric hand dryers in the bathrooms to shoot hot air up our raincoat sleeves to keep from shivering. Once we got back out into the warm rain we were fine, minus our failed experimental rain booties.

As soon as the rain stopped, a steady but short-lived tailwind sailed us down a very flat road, past our first view of sunflower fields and some very swollen creeks. It had rained five inches here in the past 48 hours, and many of the corn and soybeans fields were underwater.

Shortly before entering Buhler, a glorious blue sky and the sun appeared, and we stripped off our raingear in front of a herd of beef cows swimming in a soybean field. Later an unexpected construction detour took us off-route six miles, including a ride on a highway with a shrapnel-loaded shoulder, which resulted in our second flat tire. As the tread was getting worn, I replaced it with our spare.

We arrived in Nickerson and proceeded to the IGA supermarket to pick up a few things for dinner. There Cooper found us, a very nice young man from Minnesota also riding west. He had been reading our entries in hostel and diner guestbooks and was anxious to finally meet and talk to us. Cooper also bore news from Toronto about Gill.

"Jean Marie wanted me to tell you that you owe her one for leaving Gill with the good citizens of Toronto." Apparently, he had overstayed his welcome.

We had a very nice chat, which could have gone on for hours, but he needed to do some shopping himself before the store closed and we needed to check into Hedrick's Exotic Animal Farm B & B. Unfortunately, Cooper's average daily mileage far surpassed ours, so riding together wasn't an option we considered.

Our accommodations at Hedrick's were great. The place reminded us of the "Frontier Town" theme park back in its heyday in the Adirondacks. Besides the Wild West theme, the resort had all sorts of exotic animals: camels, zebras, kangaroos, llamas, peacocks, etc. It would be a great place for our little grandson Elijah to visit as soon as he learns how to pedal a bike here.

## Day 44, July 6, Nickerson to Larned, KS, 64 miles

Before leaving Nickerson this morning, we were happy to learn of another cyclist who checked in late in the evening. We had the pleasure of meeting Derek at breakfast, a brave and adventurous young lad from Ireland. He had flown into New York City and, heading south on his bike, had intercepted the route in Vesuvius, Virginia. He was traveling alone for the most part, although at times he had connected with a group for a few days. We were also disappointed to learn that he, like Cooper, put in long days, and would probably be a town or two ahead of us before the sun set the next day.[2]

It was a beautiful day to be cruising across the Kansas countryside, although we had no services for 58 miles. Blue skies, puffy white clouds, and an occasional east wind made the miles click by with ease. The scenery was comprised mostly of corn, soybean, wheat, and a few sunflowers fields. Oil wells were getting more numerous too. There were also quite a few beef cattle; in fact a gentleman informed us that we had just missed a three mile cattle drive down the country road we were taking (as evident by the steamy cow pies we were dodging). It reminded us of our own "running of the heifers" on our dairy farm every spring down the county highway on route to the West Eaton pasture.

We arrived in Larned by mid-afternoon. Many years ago, when I was short of winter feed for my cows, I bought a load of beautiful alfalfa hay from Larned to get me through until the spring's lush grasses could sustain the herd.

After Stephanie had a major gab-fest with the lady at the visitor's center, we made our way to Wendy's to cool our parched throats with milkshakes. We also attended the evening meeting of

---

[2]   Although we met both Derek and Cooper in Nickerson, they did not meet each other until 2000 miles later, a few hundred miles from the Pacific in the state of Oregon. They ended up riding together for the last few days and enjoyed a grand celebration together upon the completion of their journey.

the Larned Rotary Club. Our next stop was the required check-in at the police station to get a permit to camp at the city park (pool included). The officer told me the main reason for the registration was to get a contact number for next of kin. In the event of a tornado ripping through town, they needed to know where to forward your remnants to. Not a comforting thought.

The wind shifted just before dusk and the aroma of the hog farm just outside of town wafted through the tent all night. Nice. Now only if we had brought nose plugs . . . .

## Day 45, July 7, Larned to Ness City, KS, 67 miles (2027 total miles)

Emotionally, this turned out to be the lowest day of our entire voyage. We were awoken by thunder, and not wanting to pack away wet camping gear, we broke camp before sunrise. Some light showers passed while eating breakfast at a diner in town. The skies continued to threaten but we arrived at Fort Larned an hour later unscathed. There we had a great tour of the restored post-civil war era fort, built by the US Army to keep "peace" between the Plains Indians and the westward expanding white man. The restoration looked so authentic that we expected the cavalry to ride in at any minute from a scouting mission.

Things began to take a turn for the worse when we quartered to the north into a stiff headwind for 18 brutal miles. There's something about a bad head or crosswind that just pissed me off! Having to work that hard on a flat or even downhill grade; I found it very frustrating. I didn't mind the challenge of an uphill; they're supposed to be hard. Anyway, this wind put me in a very foul mood. To top it off, as we approached Rush Center, a steady rain developed.

After picking up a mail drop in town, we stopped at a diner for some lunch. We were cold and wet. "Just give me some coffee and no one gets hurt," I said to myself. I really needed some coffee. Their coffee maker was broken.

The winds relented until about 10 miles from Ness City, and soon my legs began to ache again from the additional effort required. Right about then, Stephanie remarked, "Shouldn't we be going faster?"

I reached around and gave her a head slap to the helmet. Bad move.

She, until now, had actually been holding up fairly well. Now she was in tears and wanted to go home.

Upon checking in at the Derrick Inn in Ness City, I began a major sucking up. I volunteered to walk downtown to do the laundry at what turned out to be the poorest excuse for a Laundromat in the world. There was no change machine, the soap dispenser stole my first 75 cents, and most of the washing machines and all but one of the dryers were torn apart and out of order! And the one dryer that did work had a load of wet, nasty barn clothes (i.e. lots of whole grain organic matter on the link screen) in it that I had to remove. As I left disgusted, I saw a sign that someone had taped to the back of the door that summed up the experience pretty well: "Why is this place even open?"

On the way back, I picked up a pizza that I had ordered. Stephanie still wasn't speaking to me when I offered her a piece, but when she saw I was willing to sacrifice my taste buds and dignity by buying and drinking her favorite beer, Michelob Ultra, she started to come around.

Upon checking in at the Inn, the desk clerk had informed me of the presence of another cyclist, staying in the room next to ours. Normally, I would have been eager to make acquaintances. But tonight was not the time; there was still much groveling to be done. But who was this mystery cyclist, just on the other side of our wall?

## Day 46, July 8, Ness City to Scott City, KS, 57 miles

I was hoping a memorable breakfast would help put yesterday behind us, but my egg-less egg sandwich and Stephanie's airline packaged orange juice at the local diner wasn't a good start. To top it off, the "skyscraper of the plains" (a historic limestone building in Ness City) was a disappointment, turning out to be a little "short" of our expectations—a mere four stories high. But we guessed that must have qualified for a skyscraper back in 1890, when it was built.

But the weather helped as it was a very nice day for riding. Cloudless blue skies allowed for expansive and endless views of the Great Plains, with a town about every 25 miles sporting a lighthouse in the form of a massive grain elevator which guided us through the endless sea of wheat fields. Services were far and few between, so we made sure we had plenty of water and snacks. We hardly noticed the grade, but we were slowing climbing, and upon reaching Pueblo, Colorado in a few days we would find ourselves at 5000' above sea level.

## Day 47, July 9, Scott City to Tribune, KS, 48 miles

Upon leaving Scott City, we had breakfast at the Broiler, where we feasted on the world's biggest cinnamon roll—a meal in itself. The good old boys were there, shooting the daily gossip and giving the overworked waitress a hand by keeping everyone's coffee cup full.

It was another ideal day for cycling. Big puffy white clouds floated in the calm sunny skies as we continued our cruise west through America's breadbasket into Tribune and the Rocky Mountain Time Zone. Several caravans of custom harvesters pulling huge grain combines passed us on their way to yet unharvested wheat here in the western part of the state.

On the way we met Mark, on a fully loaded bike headed to Maine. Starting in San Francisco, he had swung down into Utah to explore Zion and Bryce Canyon National Parks. He had just lightened his load by shipping his hiking backpack home. We swapped a few reflections on our journeys thus far.

The skies were buzzing with low flying crop-dusting planes today. We enjoyed the antics of one pilot as he swooped over us as he made his U turns for each new pass (being a certified applicator he was kind enough to momentarily turn off his spray each time).

Tribune is about as "country" as a town can get. When we first arrived, we thought it peculiar that every pickup truck we passed was playing the same radio station very loudly. Soon we realized that the music was originating from speakers that were mounted on each light post on the village streets.

We swam, showered, and set up camp all at the city park. Later we went multi-tasking at the truck stop: eating pizza and drinking beer while washing our clothes at the Laundromat (which was located *in* the truck stop! Only in America!)

**"I promise I'll pedal harder tomorrow if you get me a motel room
tonight?" Camping in the City Park in Tribune**

# CHAPTER 7

## COLORADO

*Highest at Hoosier*

<u>Day 48, July 10, Tribune, KS to Eads, Colorado, 61 miles</u>

We were up at the crack of dawn, and it was cool enough that we required our arm and leg warmers to insulate our goose bumps. We did not need them for long however, as temperatures quickly climbed under sunny skies to a high of 90. But the humidity had stayed relatively low during the past week, so we had been much more comfortable.

Sixteen miles into the ride we stopped to celebrate and photo-document our entrance into Colorado. The landscape was getting drier and even more desolate as we headed west, with scrubby rangeland beginning to replace the wheat fields. We slowly climbed to an elevation of 4200' today, providing us with some endless vistas, especially to the north.

In Sheridan Lake we met two groups of cyclists. Jeff and his young daughter Rebecca had begun their tour in Arizona on a tandem. Jeff's wife Gayle had started with them also but was forced off her bike by a case of heat stress encountered on their way to the Grand Canyon. She had conceded to provide SAG with the family car. Their ambitious plans were to head south after Richmond, Virginia and then to return to Arizona via a southern route, finishing around Christmas time.

Arriving in Eads in the heat of mid-afternoon, we quickly found the city pool but were unsuccessfully in cooling off in the lukewarm water. Later as a thunderstorm approached, we took shelter at the local diner where we refueled with the salad bar, dinner and pie.

Just as we were about to leave the diner, Monica, a young cyclist from Sweden, came up to us and asked if we owned the tandem outside. She had started her ride in San Francisco, traveled through Utah, and was now headed east on the TransAm. A very brave girl indeed to be traveling alone by bike in a foreign country. She had just met Dolores, a resident of Eads who was taking her out to dinner and putting her up for the night.

We stalled long enough at the diner until the skies finally cleared. Stephanie and I then made camp in the city park next to the mountain of bumper-crop wheat which had been stockpiled; the elevators had overflowed. The endless procession of grain trucks coming in to unload that night kept us awake until 10:00 PM.

### Day 49, July 11, Eads to Ordway, CO, 65 miles

Another beautiful day for riding; the plains had been good to us. We were fortunate to have nothing more than a slight crosswind to deal with—in fact we had been surprised to learn that the prevailing winds in Kansas during the summer months usually come from the south or even the southeast. The mule deer prancing down along the railroad tracks outside of Eads seemed to be enjoying the weather too.

We rode 57 miles between services today, and although we had filled our extra one gallon jug with water, we were fortunate to run into a family from Covington, Ohio just as we drank our last drops. Steve was riding east with his two sons. Kim and their two daughters were providing SAG in a van. They were kind enough to offer us snacks and water. We immediately connected as Steve was wearing an Ohio State jersey, where our son Matthew went to school. We also learned that they loved to vacation in Lake Placid, New York, just a few miles from our hometown. In fact, both Steve and his wife Kim had participated in the Lake Placid Ironman event several times, which meant they had actually cycled right past our house (on the Ironman route) many times. We plan on being out in front of our house next year to cheer them on as they ride past.

We also met Richard from New Zealand, traveling solo and fully loaded, finishing up a trip he had started last summer (from San Francisco). His final destination was Miami, Florida. A patriotic gentleman about our age, Richard flew a dozen little New Zealand flags on his handlebar bag and inside of it he revealed a transistor radio playing music (old school—no IPod for him).

Six miles before Ordway and again out of water, we pulled into tiny Sugar City (population 279) praying for something to be open (it was Sunday), and there it was, the Sugar City Diner! We quenched our parched throats with ice-cold drinks and added ice cream sundaes for good measure. One other interesting note, we figured it had now been ten days and 550 miles since we had last seen a McDonald's restaurant. Try doing that without driving on any dirt roads. We just loved pulling into a small town and finding a thriving local diner filled with friendly people, anxious to tell us about their town. Usually there was a table with the regulars, talking about the wheat harvest, yesterday's hydraulic fluid leak on the tractor, and who was going on vacation.

Today's scenic highlights included:

1.  Miles and miles of wide open rangeland, with 200 gazillion grasshoppers jumping through it and our spokes. A few beef cattle hanging out here and there around the waterholes.
2.  25 miles of Union Pacific cattle cars sitting on the railroad tracks (that we had been paralleling for several hundred miles). We figured that was at least 2500 rail cars. Sponge Bob and Plankton were painted on one. A few of the cars had side panels kicked out, obviously the work of some yahoo heifers not looking forward to becoming sirloin steaks. Later we learned that these cars were in storage, and that the tracks that they sat on had been rented for this purpose.
3.  The "Front Range" of the Rocky Mountains off on the western horizon! By now we were ready for more scenery than the plains had to offer!

Day 50, July 12, Ordway to Pueblo, CO, 54 miles

> Pueblo? I am sure you will be swinging by the Federal
> Citizen Information Center
> http://www.pueblo.gsa.gov/

> Mike, here are some sample publications that I have selected for you.
> —Pet Turtles: A Common Source of Salmonella.
> —How to Get a Job in the Federal Government.
> —Tandem Bike Touring. Five Ways to Tell If You Have a Stoker Stalker.
> —Taking Your Tent on Vacation. 15 B/B Suggestions.
> —Milkshakes. The Hidden Dangers Revealed.
>
> Have fun!! John M.
> (Blog comment)

During the night, a nasty thunderstorm blew through Ordway, but our trusty tent held up especially well; it was still in the stuff sack in the corner of the hotel room. By dawn the skies were clear, and we were on the road with our trusty "steed" by 8:30 AM.

With easy grades and light headwinds, we had covered the distance to Pueblo by early afternoon. The welcoming committee of prairie dogs stood at attention along the shoulder of the highway the last few miles into town, and the Front Range loomed close enough to make out a few patches of snow.

Our first stop in Pueblo was the bike shop, where I traded in my shredded gloves for a new pair. Our Burley Duet tandem had been running great, so there was no need to hang around for any service. After rehydrating at the bottomless soda fountain at McDonald's, we went in search of and found our first "Warmshowers" host of our trip, Ryan. *Warmshowers*.org is a website for reciprocal hospitality for touring bicyclists. This was to be our first of several stays made possible by utilizing this wonderful service, which helped us connect more with local people and bond with other cyclists.

Ryan was quite an avid cyclist (the bike tire picture frames were the giveaway) and advocate of a bike-friendly Pueblo. He did not own a car and did everything with his bike, such as commuting to work and on his days off pulling his boogie-board down to the river with a trailer. He also kept a website all about cycling including riding events which he organized and promoted around town.

Later Ryan's girlfriend Jessica joined us and the two treated us to a wonderful cookout. She was from Saranac Lake, New York, a village near us, and we discovered that we shared some common acquaintances.

Day 51, July 13, Pueblo, CO, 0 miles

Ryan was kind enough to let us stay a second day so that we could take a much needed rest and explore Pueblo's revitalized downtown, featuring a beautiful river walk, complete with Venetian-like gondola rides. After a delicious lunch of authentic Mexican fare, Stephanie and I took in the El Pueblo History Museum, which offered great exhibits on the diverse blend of cultures that shaped the city's early settlement.

Day 52, July 14, Pueblo to Royal Gorge, CO, 60 miles

Unable to locate a promising diner on our way out of Pueblo, we settled for a poor excuse of a breakfast at the Loaf and Jug Convenient Store, which featured some rather dry Danish pastries washed down with some watery coffee. Soon we were headed west along the Arkansas River, where a strong crosswind started blowing out of the north, sending tumbleweeds blowing across the road at us. The weather calmed as we entered Wetmore, where we stopped at the post office to mail out some books, maps, souvenirs, and an Elmo doll that Stephanie had picked up for Eli.

During the eleven mile downhill into Florence, the scrubby vegetation started to green up, and we caught views of Pike's Peak to the northeast. Soon we found ourselves on a busy highway to Royal Gorge, a popular spot for families on summer vacation. We passed a billboard advertising Santa's Workshop, but not the one familiar to us in Wilmington, New York. This one was in Colorado Springs, where apparently Santa has found cheaper labor and tax incentives.

We camped for the night at the KOA near Royal Gorge, where we enjoyed a few laughs with the staff and were lulled asleep by a singing cowboy who strummed his guitar by a campfire nearby.

**"Where the hell is my clean underwear?"**
**Our organizational skills are put to the test at Royal Gorge KOA**

<u>Day 53, July 15, Royal Gorge to Guffey, CO, 25 miles</u>

Fantastic weather and views eased the hardship of today's climb of 3000'. It was to be the first of several days of serious climbing which would take us over the pinnacle of our route at Hoosier Pass. The countryside had turned park-like, with more greenery than at the lower elevations we'd been at, featuring pine and scrub oak forests interspersed with grassy meadows full of wildflowers. By early afternoon we were taking the one mile detour off-route to find Guffey, elevation 8660', our destination for the night. There we found what at first appeared to be a ghost town. Almost all of its buildings were old, sheathed with weathered, slab-wood siding. There was not a soul in sight! We parked the bike in front of the local watering hole, and upon finding an "open" sign wandered in to find a couple of pleasant employees. We enjoyed great BBQ pork sandwiches and Coronas for lunch. The bartender then informed us that we could find Charlie, the caretaker of the Historic Cabins/Campground (our accommodations), at the "Garage." Surely enough, out in front of this dilapidated service station (the old pick-up truck still up on the lift dated it back to 1950) was a laid-back gentleman eager to assist us and to disseminate the history of the hamlet.

The town was populated in the 1800's when a land speculator started a rumor of a gold strike in the hills around town, although none was ever found. The three dozen houses or so were all that was left. However, most of them seemed to be occupied at least part of the year, and the town had an operating school, two bars, a post office, and a café.

Charlie continued, "Each year on the Fourth of July, the annual Chicken Flying Contest draws close to 4000 people to this quirky little town. Kids stuff each live chicken in a mailbox fitted with a door on each end. Then the birds are "encouraged" to fly by inserting a toilet plunger into one end. Things get really lively when the occasional chicken veers off-route and into the crowd!"

We soon had our tent erected in the "campground" (we passed on the little "Historic Cabins"—too claustrophobic) whose grounds were interestingly decorated with everything from a full-sized paddy wagon (with the skeleton outlaw being pulled by the skeleton of a horse) to a life-sized poster of Elvira. On our way to showering at the "Honeymoon Suite," we stopped at Rita's Café/Art Gallery, where we sipped chai teas and lattes (try finding that combination in Kansas) while I used their internet access to do some housekeeping chores.

**Guffey**

Afterwards we strolled over to the post office where we were pleased to find our mail-drop from home. The postmaster wanted to know if we knew anything of a guy named "Gill" whom she had been holding a package for which was beginning to collect dust. "Don't hold your breath!" we chuckled, filling her in on his leisurely pace. Outside we met a woman who informed us of her participation in the original BikeCentennial, which featured a layover in Guffey back in 1976. She was so smitten by the little town that she returned to live here after her coast to coast ride was over.

Later in the evening, as we were just getting ready to head back to the bar for some dinner, a lone cyclist walking his bike into the campground caught our eye. Much to our disbelief, we recognized Derek, the young Irishman who we had enjoyed breakfast with ten days ago in Nickerson, Kansas! We had figured him to be in Wyoming by now based by his daily mileage. We were so glad to see a familiar face, and in no time we were catching up on each other's adventures over dinner.

Derek had been forced to take some time off due to a knee ailment shortly after we met him in Kansas. He detoured south of Pueblo to a farm run by some friends where he took some necessary R and R. While there he helped them with their chores, and in return they had transported him and his bike back up to Florence to pick up the route. Now a couple of days back into his ride, Derek said the knee was doing OK as long as he did some stretches that a nurse had prescribed. We also learned that he in fact had been the mystery cyclist adjacent to our motel room at where else but the "Derrick Inn!"

Returning from dinner we crossed paths with some mule deer leisurely strolling through town, and then bumped into Charlie again, who we learned, as acting curator of the Guffey Museum, was authorized to give us the key to partake in a self-guided tour of its bizarre collection of oddities. Antique curiosities, busts of famous aliens, and a skeleton riding on what was claimed to be the original rocket from the movie "Dr. Strangelove" were just a few of the notable pieces.

As we retired to our tent (and Derek to his solitary confinement cabin) we were treated to a beautiful aquamarine and pink sunset, a grand exclamation point to an unforgettable, funky town.

## Day 54, July 16, Guffey to Fairplay, CO, 46 miles

Before leaving Guffey, we managed to enjoy an audience with its mayor, a black cat named "Monster." Charlie had been hopeful that he would take time off from his "campaigning" around town (mouse hunting) to stop in for a visit.

Although the grades were gradual, a steady headwind made for a very tiring day. Derek rode alongside of us most of the day, content with our slower pace to avoid aggravating his knee. The snow-capped peaks of the Rockies appeared to the north as we crested Currant Creek Pass (elevation 9404') early in today's ride. We also passed many cattle ranches, some with buildings beyond repair from a forgotten time.

**Currant Creek Pass**

Just before entering the small crossroads of Hartzel, we crossed paths with the Great Divide Mountain Bike Route. The GDMBR is another gem of the Adventure Cycling Association, featuring the 2500 miles between the Canadian and Mexican borders. The route links together a mix of everything from paved, jeep and dirt roads, single-track, to abandoned railway beds as it winds its way along the backbone of North America. One must be prepared not only for the rugged conditions but for its remoteness; only limited services are provided by the towns it passes through, which are separated by a ride of two or three days. We would intersect it approximately ten times over the next few weeks as we also followed the Continental Divide northward on the paved roads of the TransAm route.[3]

We stopped in Hartzel to enjoy a hearty lunch—complimented by chocolate malt shakes (Derek's favorite). Before pushing back into the wind, we bought a whole bag of ice from a convenient store to refill our water bottles.

In Fairplay, elevation 10,000', we began looking for a soft bed for the night, but had a difficult time finding a vacancy as motels were booked solid due to a music festival in nearby Alma. Finally we located and shared a room with Derek at the grand old Valiton Hotel. The rustic building had been rebuilt in 1922 in "Adirondack" Architecture (featuring open beams, logs, rock, and lots of antlers) after a fire had destroyed the original inn.

We gathered up Derek's and our sweaty clothes, and I helped Stephanie get them into a washer at the Laundromat. Then I found the post office and picked up another box of supplies our kids had shipped from home (which included our previously rejected long johns now needed for the increasingly cool evenings). Derek and I scouted out our options for dinner and we settled on dining alfresco at a great Italian place a few blocks away. There were also numerous souvenir shops in town, as this part of Colorado was known as South Park, and one could find trinkets of all kinds enamored with characters from the popular TV show of the same name.

---

[3] To catch the spirit of the Great Divide Mountain Bike Route, we highly recommend the independent film *"Ride the Divide"*

I'd been worried about our bike holding up, carrying the two of us and all of our gear 4000 plus miles. So tonight I performed a test to locate any stress cracks in the frame. Here were the step-by-step instructions in case you wish to do it on your own bike:

1. Purchase a bike manufactured near or at sea level.
2. Ride bike up to 10,000' above sea level.
3. WEARING SAFETY GLASSES, carefully loosen one of the water-bottle cage screws on the down-tube.
4. If screw pops out followed by hissing air, frame is good.

## Day 55, July 17, Fairplay to Breckenridge, CO, 22 miles

After a continental breakfast at the hotel, we said goodbye to Derek; he had his sights set on Silverthorne, while we had made arrangements to stay with a Warmshowers host in the upscale ski-town of Breckenridge. The first five miles out of Fairplay were on a slightly bumpy bike path, but it was a nice alternative to the highway, congested with heavy traffic on-route to the music festival in Alma. There we stopped at a coffee shop and had a pleasant chat with a middle-aged couple cycling west to east, pulling fully-loaded trailers. She was just a tiny thing, but they were celebrating their conquest of Hoosier Pass, which was now in full view just to the north of town. The pass would be only our first of nine crossings of the Continental Divide before we were done with the Rockies.

As we began our assault on the four mile climb, we had to deal with the debris left along the shoulder of the highway from the recent burying of utility lines: a foot high ridge of loose gravel right along the white line, leaving us no room to escape traffic on a very busy two lane road. We took many rests during the nerve-racking, leg-fatiguing ascent. After a punishing hour and a half, we were overjoyed to see the summit rest area come into view as we rounded one last bend in the road. At 11,542' it was the highest elevation we would reach on our voyage. We met many other cyclists at the top sucking wind. Among them were Joelle and Clyde who had started in Neskowin, Oregon on May 24th, the very same day we had left from Virginia—their home and destination. They, like us, were riding to celebrate a wedding anniversary (their 20th).

**Claude and Joelle**

Having crossed the Continental Divide, the next four miles were payback time: a screaming descent full of switchbacks and hairpin curves—thank goodness for our rear drum brake! The downhill continued but eased in gradient all the way into Breckenridge, where Stephanie was anxious to explore the many shops and restaurants in the very touristy village. But first we checked in with busy Annette, our Warmshowers host. We caught her in between shifts from working at a gift shop in town. She supplied us with ice tea, a comfy guest room, access to her washer/dryer, and a list of points of interest in the village—which included a monument to the boys of the 10th Mountain Division. Many of these unique soldiers, who fought on skis during WWII, pioneered the downhill ski industry upon their return to civilian life.

### Day 56, July 18, Breckenridge to Kremmling, CO, 58 miles

Before leaving Breckenridge, we made a carbo-loading stop at Daylite Donuts (finally, one that was open!) followed by a free ride on the gondola, which offered an aerial tour showcasing all of the condos that inhabit the mountainside.

A mostly downhill day took us through more beautiful mountain scenery under blue skies as we entered the North Park of Colorado. Bike paths between Breckenridge and Silverthorne were a welcome relief from the heavy weekend traffic, although a few more signs in Frisco would have made it much easier to follow. After battling a headwind for a while, the skies began to darken and we thought it urgent that we sought shelter. We found it in a gracious woman's garage, just before the thunderstorm hit. Eventually Marcie came out to chat with us while we waited for the storm to blow over. She was actually from West Virginia and was out visiting and taking care of her daughter who was recovering from appendicitis. Marcy's husband Ron was unable to accompany her, which was unfortunate as we would have had plenty to talk about—as he was another competitor in the annual Lake Placid Ironman Race.[4]

---

[4]   We reconnected with Ron and Marcy the following summer when they stayed with us for a few days leading up to the competition in Lake Placid. There Ron realized his life-long dream of qualifying for the Ironman Championships in Kona, Hawaii by winning his age class at 65 years young.

After crossing the bridge over the Colorado River (just a "few" miles upstream of the Grand Canyon), we pulled into Kremmling, re-hydrated at the Quickie-Mart, and made some inquiries with the cell phone regarding lodging options in town. When we rolled our bike into the storage room at the very economical Hotel Eastin, we immediately recognized Derek's bike. Soon we were dragging him out of his room and subjecting him to one of Stephanie's painfully slow shopping sprees at a grocery store. Besides needing goodies for tomorrow's 60 mile ride without services, we picked up some Fat Tire beer and munchies. We partied in the hotel lobby, reminiscing about our good times so far. We also chatted with the delightful hotel owners Danka and Jozef, a young couple who had emigrated from Slovenia, and who were nice enough to keep their front desk PC on a radio station which streamed non-stop American golden oldies from the 50's and 60's.

## Day 57, July 19, Kremmling to Walden, CO, 62 miles

The morning broke cold and rainy. We had planned on riding with Derek, but he seemed to be enjoying his soft mattress too much. We left a message with Danka for him to catch up on the road. In an hour the showers had ended, the sun was warming us, and a steady tail wind was propelling us up and over Muddy Pass, elevation 8772', our second crossing of the Continental Divide. There we stopped for lunch and to enjoy the beautiful views, including the namesake spires of "Rabbit Ears" Pass, two rocky protrusions just a few miles away. Tucked in between groves of Aspen were meadows of wildflowers in their glory; among others blue lupines and red Indian paintbrush.

Then it was a mostly downhill 35 miles to Walden, passing ranches in the North Park with 360 degree mountain views. On the way we caught up to and introduced ourselves to Dave and Carole, a couple about our age riding single bikes, also doing the TransAm east to west. Carole's bubbly personality was evident immediately, and they were by far the friendliest and most cheerful cyclists we had met on our trip. After a nice visit, we informed them that we planned to camp in the Walden city park that night (along with Derek—who we still hadn't seen yet) and would love to continue the conversation over dinner together in town.

Arriving in Walden, we began fielding the usual questions from intrigued motorists outside the convenient store, when the now increasingly common late-afternoon Rocky Mountain thunderstorm began brewing. As strong gusty winds turned the town into a dustbowl, we took refuge at the local library, where I used the internet access to update our blog and Stephanie did some money management on-line. We were glad to have gotten on the road early in the morning.

After a brief downpour, the storm blew over and we ventured over to the city park to set up camp. Refreshed by the nearby municipal pool, we rode down a few blocks to the Laundromat. No sign of Dave and Carole or Derek yet. We figured they must have holed up somewhere to wait out the storm. Then just after feeding the washing machine a half dozen quarters, we spotted Derek pedaling up to the convenient store. I ran across and told him if he hurried he could throw some clothes in with ours. Receiving those, I directed him to the park, and invited him back to meet us at the nearby Moose Creek Café for dinner. We never did see Dave and Carole that night, and assumed they had opted for a motel in town (possibly drying out from getting caught in the storm). We hoped to catch them on the road again tomorrow.

# CHAPTER 8

# WYOMING

*Parks, Pronghorn, and Prevailing Winds*

### Day 58, July 20, Walden to Saratoga, WYOMING, 70 miles

Derek treated us to a tasty breakfast at the Moose Creek Café; this trip would have definitely been a little tougher to bear without the domestication of chickens and pigs. Our waitress seemed very intrigued by Derek and asked him lots of questions, and it turned out she was gathering information for a love-struck, single, but very shy cook who had overheard his Irish accent.

We pedaled out of Walden under grey skies with cool temperatures. We were at the Wyoming border in no time, thanks to a gentle tail wind and easy grades. Soon the sun came out, and we shed a layer. Our views included the beautiful Snowy Mountain Range to the east and an endless horizon to the north. Unfortunately, it also included large tracts of dead pines, victims of the Mountain Pine beetle. The Forest Service was allowing salvage logging of these forests, which at least was helping the local economy (judging by the number of logging trucks we had seen).

Derek

We suffered puncture number three just as we pulled up to Derek, who had momentarily gotten ahead of us but was waiting at the top of a long climb. We fixed the flat tire while chatting with a solo east-bound cyclist, whom we exchanged tips on upcoming services. Later we passed a historical marker for the Overland Trail. It stated that it was last used in the 1860's, but judging by the fresh ruts, it looked as if the old stage line was still being used by the local ranchers with their turbocharged Prairie Schooners. We were pedaling in the valley of the North Platte River, a main thoroughfare for many of the historic trails of westward migration.

After a nice lunch at the Bear Trap Cafe in Riverside, Derek encouraged us to follow him the additional 18 miles to Saratoga, where we again shared a hotel room, this time at the Riviera, and feasted on take-out pepperoni pizza. We never did see our new acquaintances from yesterday, Dave and Carole.

## Day 59, July 21, Saratoga to Rawlins, WY, 46 miles

We bid adieu to Derek after breakfast in Saratoga, as he had decided to take a day off and continue to enjoy what he declared to be "the most wonderful bed in all of America." It better had been with its $90 per night price tag. We had already made reservations at a campground in Rawlins for the night. We were not sure if we would connect with him again, if not, we would miss him. By the end of the week he would be turning off route in Jackson Hole to meet a friend in Oregon.

We saw plenty of wildlife today. First, two male elk in velvet right in downtown Saratoga, then two mule deer bucks near our campground in Rawlins, and too many pronghorn antelope to count in between. And let's not forget the prairie dog, prairie chicken, rattlesnake, and the occasional coyote road kill.

We covered the first 21 miles in ludicrous speed thanks to a nice tailwind from the south. Then we tacked 90 degrees to the west onto Interstate 80 (yes, interstate as in exit ramps and tandem tractor-trailers and 75 mph speed limits). Stephanie was freaking out over the noise and suction created by the tractor-trailers passing by. I was more annoyed by a foe in the form of a nasty crosswind. The last 25 miles took twice as long.

In this part of Wyoming, with its wide open tree-less terrain, the winds seemed to be constantly blowing. Miles and miles of tall, sturdy wooden snow fence paralleled most of the roads we saw, to reduce the danger of drifting snow in the wintertime. We soon got back into a routine of starting early in the morning when the winds were usually the calmest.

After exiting the interstate, we rode past the oil refinery in Sinclair. I was disappointed in the lack of a giant green Brontosaurus out front, although there were antelopes grazing all around it on the sage-covered range.

A few miles before Rawlins, we spotted two cyclists up ahead. We spun fast and furiously to catch up. Much to our surprise and pleasure, it was Dave and Carole! It had been two days since we first met them, and by this time in our journey we had longed to finally hang with another cycling couple. Stephanie mentioned to them that today was my 52nd birthday, and during our roadside visit Carole interjected every two minutes to wish me a happy birthday. Unfortunately, we had both made previous reservations for the night, theirs at a cheap motel, and ours at the KOA (for two nights—Stephanie really needed a day off the saddle). We said goodbye, assuming that we would be at least a day behind them when we got back on the road in two days.

Upon reaching Rawlins we headed to Murray's Bike Shop to pick up a few items. Soon a nasty thunderstorm was pounding the town with buckets of a cold wind-driven rain and severe lightning. The proprietor was kind enough to let us sit it out on her couch, and luckily she had a fine collection of Adventure Cycling magazines to help pass the time. After about an hour of good reading, there was a break in the weather and we headed out to find our campground. Unfortunately, storm #2 was upon us in no time and as we looked for cover we discovered the town was without power and therefore all businesses had closed their doors. The enclosed drive-thru at the bank would have to serve as a shelter and viewpoint to watch the storm rage across the vast Wyoming landscape. In a half hour it was over, and when power was soon restored we warmed our chilled bodies with hot pizza and coffee at the nearby Pizza Hut.

## Day 60, July 22, Rawlins, WY, 0 miles

The wind blew even stronger today. We were glad to sit this one out. We visited the old Wyoming State Penitentiary, where we took a guided tour and heard all the gruesome stories of the thirteen executions, escapes, riots, and horrid conditions. There were also tales of unexplained paranormal activity ever since the "Pen" was closed in 1980. Next was the Carbon County Museum, where we were pleased to discover the long-awaited barbed wire collection.

We couldn't help but think of Derek, out in the gale battling his way west from Saratoga. We received this e-mail from him later:

> "Hey guys, only made it as far as Rawlins today. Worst day yet. The headwind was a nightmare and then got a puncture at Sinclair. Patched it but wouldn't hold the pressure, then the valve came out when trying to pump it again. Spare tubes wouldn't fit either. Then [the]bike fell over and cracked my helmet the whole way through. Arrrgggghhh. I'll see ye on the road tomorrow."

## Day 61, July 23, Rawlins to Muddy Gap, WY, 46 miles

We rose early but the winds had too. Early in the day we crossed the Continental Divide for the third and fourth time, both occurring at non-dramatic heights of land. We also rode for fifteen unbelievably straight and flat miles across the Great Divide Basin (sort of like the Bonneville Salt Flats without the salt). In Lamont, we stopped at Granny's Café, but when we found it closed we had to settle for an emergency ration of tuna salad pre-mix on pita bread (we later learned from Dave and Carole a simple knock on the door would have aroused Granny and earned us a few pancakes). As we ate, a lone cyclist approached, and we were pleased when we recognized Derek. Together we rode the rest of the way into Muddy Gap, which was no more than a crossroads with a convenient store.

Our only lodging option for the night was the "campground" behind the store. For $15 we had our choice of two sites: A, the thick prickly sagebrush around the perimeter of the parking lot or B, a concrete pad out behind the store. We chose B, mainly because it sheltered us from the constant wind, which was letting us know it wasn't quite finished with us yet by noisily flopping around pieces of the store's loose tin roofing. There were no showers, and bathrooms were to be available only when the store was open.

While hanging out at the "campground" that afternoon we met seven other cyclists, all headed east. We had a nice story telling session with them and did the mandatory swapping of advice on good places to stay and eat up ahead. All but one eventually headed on to Lamont, where they had hopes of finding better accommodations. Ernie, who was cycling the Great Divide Mountain Bike Route, decided to stay with us. On his hard-tailed bike he carried minimal equipment, including a bivy sack in place of a tent. After a good night's sleep on a piece of discarded cardboard as his sleeping pad, Ernie would re-supply at the store in the morning and head back out on the route's desolate trails.

## Day 62, July 24, Muddy Gap to Lander, WY, 82 miles

By 7:00 AM the next morning, (the posted opening time of the store), Stephanie was pacing back and forth by the locked door, with contorted looks on her face, in urgent need of a bathroom. At 7:30 she began blowing her anti-dog attack whistle in desperation, and before long the owners (who lived upstairs) were awake and unlocking the door. She practically knocked it off the hinges to get to the ladies room.

The wind gods relented today. Not even a whisper of a breeze. We were careful not to comment on this fact between ourselves, afraid that we might jinx our good fortune.

Today we rode along the Sweetwater River, in whose valley one can still find the ruts of wagon wheels from the days of the Oregon, Mormon, and Pony Express Trails (all of which converged here). We took a break at Split Rock, a navigational landmark visible for miles which guided the pioneers on their way westward. Our progress was slowed by the fact that I rarely passed on a historical marker (an addiction I inherited from my mother). One of the benefits of traveling by bicycle was going slow enough to safely pull off to read them! Needless to say they were in abundance along this stretch of highway. So many if fact, that at one of these stops, Stephanie, giving me the stink eye moaned, "At this rate, we'll meet the same fate as the

Donner Party!" I was forced to implement the "historical marker to be read later" policy, taking pictures of the signs to be viewed later.

At Sweetwater Station, we received an education on Mormon history. The campground and interpretive center told of the historic pilgrimage to the Great Salt Lake made by over 70,000 Mormon pioneers. Today young adults of the Church perform an annual reenactment, camping along the trail each summer, pulling handcarts as did their ancestors.

As we approached the crest of a glorious five mile downhill, we turned off at an overlook. Visible on the horizon was the Wind River Range, and some of Wyoming's impressive red rock country. Halfway downhill we put our brakes to the test to stop and meet rookie tandem cyclists Anna and Patrick, a young couple on their maiden voyage. They were headed east to Rawlins, where friends would pick them up and take them back to Portland, Oregon where they had started. As wise old tandem-tourers, we felt obliged to give them a few tips, but they seemed to be doing great on their own.

We were treated to a slight tailwind the last fifteen miles into Lander, helping us set a new single-day mileage record (82—a record that would stand for the rest of the trip). However, on the last hill into town, we did suffer our fourth puncture. The first on the front, it helped relieve Stephanie's building paranoia from flats occurring exclusively in the rear. We were still traveling on the original front tire and tube after almost 3000 miles of loaded touring. We were impressed by the durability of our Schwalbe Marathons; their sidewalls seem to hold up very well under the extra weight of a tandem.

Leaving Muddy Gap shortly before us this morning, Derek had warned us that he would possibly push on past Lander today, anxious to get to San Francisco in time to catch his pre-booked airline flight. We would never catch up to him again. Stephanie feared that her whistle-blowing antics had scared him off. However, little did we realize that in a room at the other end of our motel that night slept Dave and Carole, with whom we would spend some of the most memorable days of our trip during the next couple of weeks.

## Day 63, July 25, Lander to Dubois, WY, 72 miles

We survived an extremely exhausting day, consisting of 2000' of climbing compounded by a tough headwind encountered during the last 30 miles. Due to non-existent services, we couldn't make the day any shorter. Eight hours in the saddle made for two very sore butts.

According to our map, the hamlet of Crowheart was our only hope of finding a store for more fluids. When we spied Crowheart Butte off to the north (which Stephanie remarked looked more like a volcano) we knew we were getting close. Sure enough, we found a general store, and as we pedaled up, we noticed a crowd of people assembled outside, and sitting on a bench was the main attraction: Dave and Carole. Here they had held an audience captive for an hour with stories of their adventures. We were happy to see each other, and we discussed our lodging options near Dubois. Later we camped with them just shy of town, at Longhorn Campground on the banks of the Wind River. Climbing the last hill before the campground, we had a great view of some beautiful red mountains, which were made more spectacular by the shadows and soft light of the late afternoon sun.

**Red Rock. Note souvenir license plate under water jug on front rack**

## Day 64, July 26, Dubois to the base of Togwotee Pass, 26 miles

I had promised Stephanie an easy day, just to the near side of Togwotee Pass, to recover from the two previous marathons. Dave and Carole broke camp very early, as their destination was a motel on the far side of the pass. In Dubois, we enjoyed a leisurely breakfast at the popular Cowboy Café. Afterwards, while Stephanie browsed for souvenirs in the many shops lining the board-walked streets, I studied our maps and planned for the next few days.

Around midday we arrived at Lava Mountain RV Resort/ Campground, where we checked into a cabin. While cleaning and lubing the chains on the bike, I detected some sloppiness in the rear wheel bearings and upon dissection discovered that the retaining screw holding the cassette hub had worked loose. Luckily, this time we had in our possession the correct sized allen wrench to tighten it (I had picked one up after the fiasco in the Breaks). And since most of the ball bearings in the axle fell out in the process of tightening the hub, I took the opportunity to regrease both front and rear wheel bearings (luckily the camp store had some grease, however a real mountain man would have shot one of the Grizzly bears that had been hanging around these parts and rendered some of its fat into grease). Carrying the necessary tools all this way had definitely paid off, as again there were no bike shops for miles around. I considered myself fortunate to have spent two summers at GUY'S BIKE SHOP IN MADISON, NY (non-paid advertisement) as an apprentice bike mechanic, where I had learned how to do this. Thanks Guy—you were a good teacher!

## Day 65, July 27, Togwotee Pass to Coulter Bay Village, WY, 44 miles

Our climb up Togwotee Pass (our fifth crossing of the Continental Divide at 9658') was shortened by three miles due to a construction zone, where we were given a mandatory lift in a contractor's pick-up truck over some rough gravel. We learned that a week ago there was such a large group of cyclists here that a flatbed trailer had been called in to ferry them through. Once the summit was reached, where the high altitude wildflowers were again spectacular, we had a glorious 17 mile downhill with postcard views of the Tetons opening up before us.

**Descending Togwotee Pass: The Tetons**

Entering Grand Teton National Park, we pulled up along the banks of the Snake River for the mandatory Ansel Adams (dubbed "Adam Anslow" by Stephanie) photo extravaganza (see cover photo). Soon we were checking in at the Coulter Bay campground, where we were directed towards the hiker/biker sites. In the National Parks, even if the campground is posted as "full," a cyclist is never turned away. As we rode through the loops to pick out a cozy site, we recognized Dave and Carole's tent. Able to track down their bikes parked outside the visitor's center, we later enjoyed an evening of great food and conversation with them—the first of several.

## Day 66, July 28, Coulter Bay to Grant Village, WY 44 miles (3014 miles total)

To avoid heavy Park traffic (i.e. the Winnebago migration), we broke camp early. Cruising along Jackson Lake, we were treated to ideal weather and more great scenery. As we rode we played cat and mouse with Dave and Carole, taking pictures of each other as we entered Yellowstone National Park. Near Lewis Falls, where our odometer hit the 3000 mile mark, we crossed the Continental Divide for the sixth time. Yellowstone had made a beautiful green recovery since the fires of 1988. We had vacationed here with my brother Chris and his children a few years after the burn at which time the scorched landscape had been somewhat depressing.

We checked in at the NP Campground at Grant Village in the afternoon, sharing a site with Dave and Carole. After pitching our tents and fluffing up our sleeping bags we had a memorable dinner with them in the restaurant overlooking Yellowstone Lake. We learned much about them that night; Dave's career had taken them all around the world. Then soon after their two children had graduated from high school, they sold their home in New Orleans and had thru-hiked the entire Appalachian Trail. They couldn't wait to have "grandbabies" as Carole called them, and were planning on settling down again when and where the first one arrived.

During their bike ride Carole had experienced some back and shoulder problems, but had the drive and willpower to never give up. There were times we had caught up to them on our daily rides when she was literally laying on the pavement to ease her pain, yet she continued to go on. Dave had the patience of a saint and was extremely supportive, he would let her set the pace: nice and easy—hence their very early starting times, frequent rests and long days.

**Dave and Carole**

We told them about our four children and new grandson, about the hardships and rewards of operating our own businesses for 25 years (while I was busy farming Stephanie operated her own flower shop). When we started in on the crazy cow stories, they reciprocated with a tale involving a pet chicken they once had. It would sit on their laps while they watched movies and help them eat the popcorn. Their children potty trained it by taping a dowel across the toilet seat, where it would roost at night.

The evening could have gone on forever, but after coffee and dessert we looked out through the window of the restaurant only to see whitecaps forming on Yellowstone Lake. After paying our bill, we hopped on the bike just as raindrops began to fall and made a frantic one mile sprint back to the campground, anxious to put a rainfly over our yet uncovered tent. With temperatures predicted to drop down into the 30's that night, we did not want to sleep in soaked sleeping bags.

## Day 67, July 29, Grant Village, WY, 0 miles

I woke up just before dawn to relieve myself, and upon taking my first step out of the tent a sudden excruciating pain in my left ankle almost caused me to fall over. After limping back to the tent, I tried to recall what I could have done yesterday to injure it. Then I remembered the mad dash back to the campground after dinner, and doing it with joints that had gotten cold and stiff from sitting for hours.

We had planned on taking a day off in Yellowstone, but with all that there was to see and do here at "Coulter's Hell," hobbling around the campground was not exactly how I had planned to spend it. I took some Ibuprofen and kept my leg elevated. Sewing a few souvenir patches on our panniers helped pass the time. Stephanie took a nap and did some reading. Dave and Carole took a "zero" day also, opting to go on a guided bus tour of the park. The most exciting event of their day wasn't a close encounter of bison or bears, but the stumble off the bus by a woman, requiring ambulance and EMT assistance.

By the evening, news had spread through the hoards of vacationers in Yellowstone that a sow grizzly bear and her two cubs had gone on a rampage, killing one camper and seriously injuring others. Luckily for us, the incident occurred at a campground at the opposite corner of the park. We also learned of two escaped and highly dangerous convicts (from a prison in New Mexico) who had been seen in the park. We were anxious to get moving.

### Day 68, July 28, Grant Village to Madison Junction, WY, 39 miles

The day of rest had done nothing for my ankle. It was now a dull but severe ache that radiated up my leg. We were puzzled, as there was no swelling or discoloration that Stephanie or I could detect. To get medical attention, we would need to ride to the clinic at Old Faithful, which was 21 miles away, which included two more crossings (the seventh and eighth) of the Continental Divide. After breakfast, we decided to give it a try. I kept the tandem in a low gear (Stephanie called it "spinning air") and surprisingly, my ankle began feeling better with each passing mile. By late morning we were at Old Faithful, where we checked in at the waiting room of the clinic. Weren't we "surprised" when the receptionist informed us that the clinic did not participate in our insurance group. We settled into some comfy waiting room chairs and began perusing through their fine collection of literature. About fifteen minutes later, I startled my wife by jumping up and throwing my copy of People magazine aside.

"What's wrong?" she exclaimed.

"Old Faithful! She's erupting! Where's that camera?" I ran outside, and finding it quickly in the handlebar bag snapped a few pictures. I was only able to get the top of the geyser—the clinic was not at ringside.

Morgan, the cute Physician's Assistant at the clinic, diagnosed me with what was basically "carpal tunnel" of the foot. By touching my toes with a vibrating tuning fork, she detected a loss of sensation, caused by the compression of nerves where they ran through my ankle.

"Soaking it in cold water at the end of each day and taking an Aleve each night before bed should subdue the symptoms," were her comforting words. We were relieved; there was no reason why we couldn't continue.

We rode a short distance to the Bear Paw Deli. Over some burgers and fries we discussed our options for the day, and I suggested trying for the Montana border at West Yellowstone; it was mostly downhill. We called ahead to get prices on campgrounds and hotels. Rather than take out a second mortgage on our house, we decided to stop at the National Park campground in Madison Junction. Dave and Carole were to stay and enjoy the grandeur of the historic Old Faithful Inn, which was also way over what our budget would allow (if they even had a vacancy). One of the last remaining log hotels in the United States, the Inn was built from materials within the park in the winter of 1903-04.

We pitched our tent at the quiet, grassy hiker/biker loop of the campground, secluded from the blacktopped cul-de-sac for RV vacationers. Later I walked down to the Gibbon River, where I soaked my ankle in its cool waters as the trout rose for the evening's fly hatch.

Before the sun set, we had the pleasure of meeting seven other cyclists who rolled in to camp. One young man from Switzerland had an unexplainable longing to get to Devil's Tower National Monument in northeast Wyoming. We noticed he was living off mashed potatoes and had a passion for sculpting them with his fork. There was an older couple from St. Louis headed west to Oregon; he wanted to reconnect with some old army buddies. The rest were a group of college students, including a girl who carried a ukulele on her bike. They planned to rent a car in West Yellowstone in the morning and take a whirlwind tour of the park.

# CHAPTER 9

## MONTANA

*Magnificent Mountains*

<u>Day 69, July 31, Madison Junction, WY to Hebgen Lake, MT, 35 miles</u>

The ladies working in the nearby campground registration booth invited us to help ourselves to their coffee maker in the morning, although we were instructed not to let the RV campers see us. Ken Burns was right! The National Parks were America's best idea.

The doctor's orders seemed to have worked as my ankle was pain free today. After the "entering Montana" photo shoot and a few errands in West Yellowstone, we reconnected with Dave and Carole at a backstreet diner that an east-bounder had tipped us off about.

The skies were darkening as we headed out of town, and after eight miles it caught up to us: a brief but nasty thunderstorm, spewing lots of gusty wind. Luckily we found shelter at a Montana Department of Transportation building. The storm blew over quickly, leaving a clear blue sky. Soon we were cycling along the shores of beautiful Hebgen Lake, a long narrow body of water tucked between two mountainous ridges.

We stopped at a campground store for some chocolate milk and a "New York Hotdog," featuring Sauerkraut and Gulden's Mustard. Oddly enough we've only been able to find "Michigan" style hotdogs back home in New York State. We were soon joined by newlyweds William and Lauren, an Australian couple cycling eastward. William's grandfather Keith had been the inspiration for their journey, having completed the BikeCentennial Ride in 1976. His adventure was documented in his book, *It's All Up Hill*, which William and Lauren carried with them and read from each night for the ultimate déjà vu experience. When Dave and Carole rolled in and joined the party, they informed the Aussie's that they had better get to work producing some grand-babies for the their parents down under.

Our nice picnic was interrupted by a passing motorist who informed us that the power lines further down the Madison River valley had been taken out by the storm. Rather than risk taking a cold shower (or none at all) at a campground without electricity, we decided to end our day early here.

### Day 70, August 1, Hebgen Lake to Ennis, MT, 53 miles

Unbeatable weather (cool and blue) and scenery along the Madison River (the fly-fisherman's paradise) made for a great day of riding. We stopped at the Quake Lake visitor's center early in the day, where in 1959 a magnitude 7.2 earthquake triggered a massive rock slide which dammed the river. The rapidly rising waters of the newly created lake killed 28 people and injured and trapped many more. At a roadside overlook of the lake, we met an older couple in an RV who told us an eerie story involving friends of theirs who were camped down by the river on the very night of the earthquake 51 years ago.

> "Around 9:00 in the evening they both woke feeling uneasy, and not being able to get back asleep, decided to pack up and leave. When the quake hit three hours later, most of the campers that remained were soon dead or seriously injured. Some higher power was looking out for them."

**Quake Lake**

Just outside of Ennis, the Montana DOT had set up a weigh station for truckers. We pulled in line with the tractor trailers, hoping these guys could accommodate us on their scales (we'd had many people inquire about the amount of weight we were carrying). They were willing but claimed we would need to balance the bike on end, so we passed on the offer. I estimated our total weight (us included) to be around 450 lbs (at the time that included a Smokey Bear plush doll / action figure that Stephanie had picked up for our grandson Elijah).

From there it was easy cycling into Ennis, where our destination was the Riverside Motel, which came highly recommended by our amateur travel agent/sister-in-law Amy. Amy is one of the "East Coast Battisti's" (hailing from Massachusetts, Maryland, and New York) which had recently met up and vacationed with the "West Coast Battisti's" (all residing in Seattle). Their trip had taken them through some of the same towns in western Montana that we were headed for.

After a double scoop Huckleberry ice cream cone in town, I did some routine bike maintenance and sewed more souvenir patches on our panniers, which were beginning to look so classy that they may have to be retired and hung up for display when we got home. Stephanie opted for the nap, as it had been seven days since our last motel and real bed.

We met Dave and Carole again for dinner. Carole was quite daring and ordered the baked bean, pulled pork and BBQ sauce pizza—which she gave a two thumbs up! Over dinner we learned that Dave was born without the sense of smell, and so his sense of taste was very limited. We had noticed that he added generous amounts of salt to his food, and consumed lots of chocolate which he said were the two things he could "taste" somewhat.

### Day 71, August 2, Ennis to Alder, MT, 24 miles

After breakfast at the Pharmacy in Ennis we headed up a big pass. We had planned on lightening our load at the Ennis post office but it wasn't due to open until an hour after we went by it. So we continued giving Smokey a lift instead of mailing him home. At an overlook halfway up, Jamie from Middlebury, Vermont and two other young collegiate cyclists caught up to us and stopped to chat. When they left to resume the climb, Stephanie and I managed to stay on their wheel almost all the way to the summit, not bad for us middle-aged farts.

After eight miles and 2000' of elevation gain we began a well-earned descent into Virginia City, a historic but very much commercialized ghost town. Gold was discovered in nearby Alder Gulch in 1863. We found the town was now very much alive and spent several hours checking out its shops and museums. One of the museum's themes was antique arcade machines, and we immediately recognized a Zoltar-like mechanized fortune teller (the one that worked when unplugged in the movie *"Big"* with Tom Hanks) which we later learned was valued at several million dollars. Later we went on a very entertaining narrated fire engine ride around town.

At a small café in Nevada City (another ghost town but less commercialized) we couldn't pass on the Huckleberry milkshakes. From there it was just a few more downhill miles to the KOA in Alder. No sign of Dave and Carole, they had pushed on to Twin Bridges, further down the Ruby River valley.

## Day 72, August 3, Alder to Dillon, MT, 50 miles

Just another beautiful day of cycling in Big Sky Country. After ten miles we stopped in Sheridan for the "sweet tooth special" breakfast at the corner bakery. From there it was another quick ten miles downhill into Twin Bridges, where we checked out the "cyclists only" campground, complete with restrooms, showers, screened in picnic area, and even a floor pump for topping off one's tires (a nice break from dealing with the mini-pumps that tourers carry). If only there was one of these every 50 miles! One cyclist had left her calling card there: the ukulele.

Then turning to the southwest and following the Beaverhead River upstream, it wasn't long before we spotted Beaverhead Rock off in the distance, the hunk of limestone that Sacagawea had recognized in 1805 as part of her tribe's home turf. No sign of Chief Cameahwait and the Shoshone Indians though, so we were unable to trade the bike for some fresh horses. Luckily Lewis and Clark had fared better.

We passed many east-bound cyclists during the day's ride, including a couple with a German accent who yelled out something as they passed. After a few seconds it dawned on us— they had yelled our names! Must be Dave and Carole were up ahead and had told them to watch for a couple on a tandem. She had given them this phrase to recite so they wouldn't forget our names: "Mike leads the bike, Stephanie's at the stern." Cute. We caught up to them later that night at Papa T's in Dillon for dinner.

## Day 73, August 4, Dillon to Jackson, MT, 49 miles

We pedaled out of Dillon after a very hearty breakfast at Sparky's Garage, where we enjoyed the ambiance of the 1950's filling station décor. We would need the calories from the greasy bacon, eggs, home-fries, and sausage gravy that slid down our throats, as we had two back-to-back passes to conquer. When we got home from this trip, we thought it wise to have a doctor check the viscosity of our blood.

Under blue skies, we began our long assault on Badger Pass. We broke up the slow but steady grind with several peanut butter and jelly-on-a-bagel sandwich breaks. Next on the agenda was Big Hole Pass. By the time we crested its summit at 7360' we were pretty well whipped. Thank goodness it was all downhill from there into the beautiful and spacious Big Hole Valley, "the Land of 10,000 Haystacks." We saw a few haystacks dotting the green, corral-fenced meadows and the odd looking "beaver slides" that made them, but today most ranchers in the valley have switched to making modern round bales of hay, or "Twinkies" as some farmers call them.

"This ain't your saddle—it's my pillow!"
**Taking a break between Badger and Big Hole Passes**

Just before entering Jackson, we passed a historical marker locating the spot where William Clark had ordered the Corp of Discovery to parboil some meat in a hot spring. Minutes later we arrived at the Jackson Hot Springs Lodge Resort/Bar/Restaurant/Campground/etc. where we checked into our cabins. Unfortunately the hot springs pool had just been refilled after cleaning, and at 140 degrees we did not care to parboil our derrieres. After a nap we rendezvoused with Dave and Carole for a fine meal and conversation at the Resort's restaurant. We were really going to miss them when our routes forked in Missoula; they were to continue on the TransAm route west through Idaho and into Oregon, whereas we were headed north to Libby to intercept the Northern Tier route.

## Day 74, August 5, Jackson to Darby, MT, 77 miles

Another stellar day to be riding a bicycle. After a short warm-up of easy spinning, we put the tandem in the big ring gear and sprinted the 18 level miles to Wisdom, where we found a nice diner. On the way we were dive-bombed by a large bird that was being protective of her chicks which were snuggling up in a nest atop a telephone pole. Breakfast was followed by another ten easy miles to the Big Hole National Battlefield, where a film and exhibits told of the sorrowful flight of the Nez Perce Indians from the US Army in August of 1877.

By late morning we were climbing the relatively easy grade along beautifully wooded Trail Creek. The road did steepen the last two miles up to the top of Chief Joseph Pass, where at 7241' we crossed the Continental Divide for the ninth and last time. During ascents of the last few passes, as our pace began to decrease, horse and deer flies would catch up to us, which occasionally resulted in a painful bite! Stephanie would take the opportunity to slap me silly, claiming that she was "just killing flies!"

After one quick downhill mile we arrived at an intersection, and while planning to turn right, we were surprised to spy a "Welcome to Idaho" sign to our left. We rode the 100 yards to the state line, took a photo, and then did a U turn. We would enter Idaho again in nine days, but much further north. Another five minutes found us at a rest area at Lost Trail Pass, where I took pictures of all the interpretive signs illustrating the Corps of Discovery's westward travels through here in the fall of 1805. The plethora of signs was enough to generate a rolling of the eyes by Stephanie—prompting me to again initiate the "read the text from the pictures later" rule.

Here at Lost Trail Pass, William Clark and a handful of men—with their "not-so-trusty" old Indian guide Toby leading the way—had split from Meriwether Lewis and the rest of the Corps of Discovery to explore the feasibility of taking the Salmon River through Idaho to connect with the Columbia. Old Toby's orienteering skills failed him, and the rough, twisting "River of No Return" lived up to its name, forcing the group to turn back and reunite with Lewis and find a more northerly overland route (at Lolo Pass).

Leaving the rest area, we began a thrilling seven mile downhill complete with switchbacks and hairpin curves! At Sula, the grade eased as we began riding along the Bitterroot River, enjoying views of snowcapped, jagged Trapper Peak and the Bitterroot Mountains.

Dave and Carole had again gotten off to an early start, and it was now our daily routine as they say in the Tour de France to "chase down the Peloton." We finally reeled them in six miles shy our evening's destination, where we found them taking a rest (she was napping by the road again).

In Darby we all stuffed our bellies at the Silver Spoon Diner, where platefuls of food smothered with gravy were washed down with milkshakes, ice water and coffee. We had planned on camping that night, but for four dollars more than a tent site, we upgraded to the "bunkhouse." We played a few hands of hearts while our communal load of laundry spun in the washing machine. Later Carole and I looked over the maps and discussed our options for tomorrow's ride. For every few days she wrote up a detailed flow chart noting upcoming distances and services depending on where they finished each night. Somewhere in the conversation I spilled the beans; if they were to go into Missoula with Stephanie and me to visit the headquarters of the Adventure Cycling Association (the touring cyclist's heaven—as in free ice cream and other useful resources) they would actually have to backtrack thirteen miles to Lolo to get back on the TransAm route to Idaho.

"What?" exclaimed Carole as she took a closer look at the map. "You know we don't go a single mile off-route for anything! I guess we'll just have to write you and Stephanie a note giving you the rights to our free ice cream!"

Oh well. One less day with Dave and Carole.

## Day 75, August 6, Darby to Lolo, MT, 55 miles

It was a quick and easy day down the Bitterroot Valley. I could only finish half of my "Spud Special" at Deb's Diner—a monumental heap of sumptuous fried potatoes, onions, peppers, and mushrooms smothered in sausage gravy and molten cheese—before rolling out of Darby (the other half made for a great picnic lunch near Florence).

We took advantage of a steady tailwind to cover 25 of the day's mileage in just less than 90 minutes. A crosswind developed however, as the wind began to swing around from the east, but the pleasure of riding the last 16 miles on a paved bike path made our cruise into Lolo pleasant just the same.

We found and entered a McDonald's for shakes and burgers. It was only midday, too early to check into the motel room we had reserved. We had not passed Dave and Carole during the ride, so Stephanie called them with our cell phone. They were still on the road, battling what was now a fierce headwind. They had been delayed in Hamilton, where they had run into difficulties at a pharmacy trying to transfer some pictures from their memory depleted digital camera.

Tonight would unfortunately be our last night to enjoy their company. We walked over to Pizza Hut for dinner where Dave, Stephanie and I all went in on a couple of pizzas while Carole ordered the family style bucket of pasta. The waitress soon brought out the food and handing Carole a large serving spoon explained, "just in case you want to share some of that pasta."

"Dream about it! You can take that spoon right back where it came from!" replied Carole. And she ate the whole thing.

Later that evening, we played cards, shared some pictures, and reminisced about our trips so far. I also gave them a few minutes of air time on our digital recorder for commentary and reflection. The next few evenings would have been awful lonely if it weren't for a date we had with a finicky piece of farm equipment to keep us occupied.

## Day 76, August 7, Lolo to Clinton, MT, 30 miles

We said our sad farewells, and Dave and Carole headed west over Lolo Pass and into Idaho. We would miss them, but hopefully not for long, as we think we may have convinced them to come and visit us at our home in the Adirondacks Mountains of New York this fall, as they had never witnessed the flaming leaves of a northeastern autumn.[5]

We had no trouble finding the Adventure Cycling headquarters in Missoula, where we spent two hours enjoying their treasure trove of all things cycling, including antique and historic bikes, maps, books, gear, clothing, and pictures—including Polaroids of all the thru cyclists who had stopped in during the summer (many of whom we recognized). Sarah and the other extremely helpful gals manning the office that Saturday also gave us some details on the upcoming leg of our journey.

After consuming a few tasty treats at the Missoula Farmer's Market, we met a very young couple on a recumbent tandem. They were from Northampton, Massachusetts and were doing a modified version of the Northern Tier route.

Continuing east, in no time we found the home of Bud and Anne in Clinton. Bud and Anne were the owners of the finicky piece of farm equipment—a hay baler. They were also the parents of Earl, an acquaintance of ours and very good friend of my brother Steve. Earl had lost a battle with cancer several years ago, and Steve and Amy had made several trips to Montana to visit his parents since his passing. Their last visit had occurred during the "Battisti family vacation/reunion of 2010" which had taken place less than a month ago. We were somewhere in Colorado when I received this call from Steve during his visit:

"Mike—we're at Bud and Anne's. Bud is having a heck of a time with the knotter on his hay baler. It's a New Holland, and it looks just like yours."

---

[5]  They did in fact come for a glorious one week reunion that very October, at the peak of our dazzling display of fall foliage, which was especially brilliant that year.

"Is it a model 273?" I asked, as I envisioned the red and yellow piece of farm machinery which had provided me with enough headaches during my career as a dairy farmer to keep Excedrin in business.

"Sure is! I'll tell them you're on your way!"

So that is how it came to be that we found ourselves headed to Clinton, a dozen miles off route, to visit a couple that we didn't know. I had called Bud and Anne a few days earlier to get some directions and to let them know when to expect us. Although Steve had told us how wonderful they were, we were still a little anxious.

They had been watching for us from their lawn chairs. Within an hour, over refreshments around the table, we felt we had known Bud and Anne all our lives. We learned that Bud had spent most of his life as a logger, and that Anne was a retired seamstress. They told great stories of their life's adventures, with their children, at work, and at their hunting camps. We were soon joined by a couple of their good friends, bearing gifts of vine-ripened garden tomatoes and cucumbers. With the addition of Ann's delicious stew, we feasted on a memorable dinner. We also had the pleasure of meeting their grandson and great-grandchildren, who joined us for dessert!

We now looked forward to a day off with them tomorrow, a day off that didn't involve pain or a broken wheel.

Day 77, August 8, Clinton, MT, 0 miles

Bud and Ann suggested we take a scenic ride in their car up around Flathead Lake, pick up some cherries which the area was famous for, and forage for some wild huckleberries. Now I knew why Steve got along with them so tremendously, they were "hunter-gatherers" just like himself!

It had been almost two months since Stephanie and I had ridden in a car, so when Bud brought his car up onto the interstate ramp and set the cruise control at 70 mph, it took our pulse rates a few minutes to return to the comfort zone. We rode through the Flathead Indian Reservation where we took in great views of the majestic Mission Mountains to the east. Along the eastern shore of Flathead Lake we found our cherries, but the famed huckleberries managed to elude us. We also did a drive-by of the annual Testicle Festival, Montana's version of the Sturgis Motorcycle rally, with the added flair of testicles roasting on an open fire.

After returning home, Anne fixed us some awesome breaded elk steaks, the best meal we'd had in months. After supper, while Stephanie and Anne took care of dishes and then watched their fill of Hallmark movies on the tube, Bud and I tinkered with his hay baler's knotter. A hay baler has more moving parts than a centipede, and somewhere on one of the knotters one of them was just out of adjustment enough to prevent it from tying a consistent knot. I made a few adjustments, proclaimed it fixed (with my fingers crossed) and we went back to our lawn chairs. With a beer in hand and a shot of Early Times at our side, we had a great evening of conversation, from farming and logging to hunting and fishing.

**Bud and Anne**

## Day 78, August 9, Clinton to Swan Lake, MT, 72 miles

With last night's leftovers Anne made us a great breakfast of elk steak burritos, and packed us three more to go. With the addition of enough fresh fruit and vegetables to make our panniers bulge at the seams, we packed up to head north. Visiting Bud and Anne had been like going to visit family; they had been so generous and welcoming, and we felt so much at ease. And they had never even met us. In return I sure hoped that baler worked good for them next summer.

Bud insisted on giving us a ride back to rejoin our route, so we put the tandem and panniers in his pickup and rode back to Milltown, where we picked up a mail drop from Melanie and Ken which included Elijah's first piece of artwork (very abstract).

We rode along the Blackfoot River, the inspiration for Norman Maclean's *A River Runs Through It*, and made a stop in Seeley Lake to see the historical society's exhibit on Norman and wife Jessie's summers spent at the family cabin on Seeley Lake (his descendants still use it to this day). Also featured in the museum were interesting exhibits on logging and the history of fighting forest fires, two of the area's more important economic activities.

Later in the afternoon we rode north, towards the headwaters of the Clearwater River, flanked on the left by the snow-capped Mission Mountains and on the right by the Swan Mountains and the Bob Marshall Wilderness—yes, the Bob Marshall of Adirondack fame. Robert "Bob" Marshall (1901-1939) was an American Forester, writer and wilderness activist. During his youth he frequently visited the Adirondacks, where he developed his affection for outdoor pursuits. He was a principal founder of the Wilderness Society, the organization which was the driving force behind the Wilderness Act of 1964 and the preservation of America's 106 million acres of federal wilderness.

After passing Summit Lake, we descended into the Swan River watershed, a beautiful chain of lakes. We followed this downstream until we found the Swan Lake Trading Post, a great full-service Mom and Pop campground. Joe checked us in and showed us all around. Later that evening after pizza in the café, Jocelyn gave me the pleasure of sampling a free piece of her experimental huckleberry-upside-down cake. I gave it five stars.

## Day 79, August 10, Swan Lake to Kalispell, MT, 38 miles

About nine miles down the road this morning we happened upon the mother-lode of huckleberry bushes, so we called Bud and Anne and gave them the exact coordinates of its location. Later as we rode west towards Bigfork, we stopped at a rise to admire a view of The Great Chinese Wall in the Bob Marshall Wilderness. Actually a portion of the Continental Divide, the massive 1000 foot escarpment runs in a north-south direction for twelve continuous miles.

In Kalispell, after grabbing a sandwich, we decided to call it a day when thunderheads began to fill the western sky. We took refuge at the Hilltop Motel, but only after we had gone on a wild goose chase to recover our cell phone.

We had noticed it missing after checking in to the motel; Stephanie had last used it on a bench at the city park to call around for motel options. I immediately hustled back to see if it was still there. By the time I arrived, a band was playing an evening concert in the gazebo, and the benches were full of people. The people sitting in our bench had not seen a phone. I headed back to the motel.

In the meantime, Stephanie had come up with the brilliant idea to go to the motel office and requested that they ring our cell phone's number, which they did. Soon she had the location of our phone; someone had found it in the park and given it to a concessionaire who was selling treats at the concert. Unfortunately, my wife couldn't inform me of this fact until I returned, so then it was her turn to walk up to the park!

## Day 80, August 11, Kalispell to Middle Thompson Lake, MT, 46 miles

After some construction just west of Kalispell, we found the historic route of the Great Northern Railroad, now a beautiful rail trail. That took us past Kila, where we turned back onto the highway and rode through some well-managed timber country. The multitude of logging trucks that passed us were all very well behaved. Soon we were at the Thompson Chain of Lakes and Logan State Park, where we made camp for the night.

The beautifully clear night was interrupted once by the wail of a loon, and the second time by the cry of my bladder. On the way to the restroom I admired the great display of stars on this moonless night. Spotting a shooting star, I then remembered it was August

11th—date of the annual Perseid meteor shower! For years on this particular evening I would drag our children outside in their pajamas and, snuggled in blankets, we would count the meteorites. Later my son Andrew, now an astronomy grad student, would write that this is what inspired his chosen field of study.

## Day 81, August 12, Middle Thompson Lake to Libby, MT, 48 miles

We were unhappy after leaving Happy's Inn (an actual place on the map), as we had to settle for microwaveable burritos for breakfast. It was another 43 miles without services into Libby and the junction of the Northern Tier route.

Just outside of town we caught our first glimpse of the impressive Cabinet Mountain Wilderness to the west. It was also a notable day for wildlife viewing; we spotted a whitetail doe and fawn, and just a few miles later a moose cow and calf crossed the road just in front of us.

We stopped at the library in Libby where Stephanie went online and purchased two airline tickets. With less than 500 miles to go, we felt safe to calculate a conservative date to fly home. Meanwhile, I sent this email to my relatives in Seattle:

> "Attention Seattle Siblings:
> We've calculated that we have at least a dozen more days of riding to Seattle, so Stephanie is in the process of booking us flights home for the 31st of August, which should give us a few days to unwind with you all! This will also include the ride to the Pacific (by then we may settle for Lake Washington or some other body of water— as long as it connects to the Pacific) and the ceremonial dipping of the front wheel into its waves! This may be followed by the ceremonial heaving of the bike off a cliff (depending on what it will cost us to ship it back home— we can't take it on the plane!)"

At this stage in the ride, Stephanie's rear end had begun to object to the long hours on the saddle, and she was in favor of the "off a cliff" option. I on the other hand was saddened by the thought of our glorious adventure coming to its end.

We settled in at the Caboose Motel and had pizza delivered. No souvenir conductor caps to be had.

## Day 82, August 13, Libby to the Confluence of the Bull and Clark Fork Rivers, WA, 51 miles

A quick eleven miles down the road found us at Kootenai Falls, where we took a short hike to check out one of the few falls on a major river in the northwest that is not dammed up for hydropower. Four miles later we turned to the south and followed along the Bull River drainage with the Cabinet Mountains this time to the east. The very scenic ride was like flipping through a rack of picture postcards, with views of wildflowers, stately evergreens, and towering mountains.

We stopped midday at Little Joe's Cafe in the middle of nowhere for lunch, where there was no sign of Hoss and the rest of the Cartwrights. I think they were out filming the episode where Ben hires some unlicensed pesticide applicators to aerial spray the Ponderosa for those pesky mountain pine beetles.

We saw our first wolf. It crossed the road a few hundred yards in front of us. Stephanie had been moaning all day about her butt being sore and I think the predator had mistaken her for a stressed out, wounded animal wanting to be put out of its misery. On second thought, I think the wolf had her pegged pretty accurately.

Before reaching our secluded campground, tucked down in a hollow by the Clark Fork River, we stopped at a convenient store to refuel with chocolate milk, and met a nice young man originally from Worchester, Massachusetts who was on a mountain bike and pulling a trailer. His adventure had started in Edmonton, Alberta and would finish in Bellingham, Washington, doing a mix of forest service and paved roads. We shared our Adventure Cycling maps with him as he was getting by with some crude computer printouts.

# CHAPTER 10

## IDAHO

*Brief but Beautiful*

### Day 83, August 14, Confluence of Bull and Clark Fork Rivers to Sandpoint, IDAHO, 51 miles

Today we arrived in Idaho (actually the official name of the state is "Udaho," as some resident with a can of spray paint had reminded us of on the welcoming sign). It would be by far our quickest state, as we were in the northern panhandle. We stopped in the town of Clarks Fork for breakfast at Mom's, our first real breakfast in five days (since our stay with Bud and Anne in Clinton). Later we rode along the north shore of very blue and big Lake Pend Oreille, which we learned was the remains of Glacial Lake Missoula. About 12,000 years ago, a 2000' tall ice dam backed up the Clark Fork River and created a lake bigger than Lakes Erie and Ontario combined. When the dam broke, it made a real mess out of eastern Washington and also carved out the Columbia River Gorge.

Our early start coupled with relatively level terrain brought us to Sandpoint before 1:00 PM. In addition we had to set our watches back an hour due to our entering of the Pacific Time Zone at the state border. So what to do for three hours before we could check into our motel? Soon we learned of a "fly in" at the airport (we had noticed the skies were very busy on the ride in) so we pedaled over to check it out. Many vintage biplanes, Pipers and Cessnas were on display and available for rides. One of my hobbies when I was a kid was building flying balsa wood model airplanes, including many of the planes that were here today. I was thrilled just to look and drool on them.

From there we continued on down to the bike shop, where we shelled out $16 for hopefully our last tube of butt butter (priced like liquid gold but these guys knew we couldn't live without it).

After a visit to the generic Dairy Queen, we made our way to the Ho-Jo's Motel where I managed to perform a six-point turn to get the fully loaded tandem into the lobby to unload. Normally we just wheeled the bike into our room, but this required scoring a room on the ground floor. Back in Newton, Kansas we did execute a second-floor check-in with the bike fully loaded, but there we had a straight shot from the door up the flight of stairs.

Once settled in, we had the ultimate "Medieval Times" dining experience: Wal-Mart rotisserie chicken in bed. The flimsy complimentary plastic knives and forks were optional (and useless). Needless to say, we employed our bath towels as bibs.

# CHAPTER 11

## WASHINGTON

*Pampered at the Pacific*

<u>Day 84, August 15, Sandpoint, ID to Newport, Washington, 40 miles</u>
A nice tail wind today allowed us to throw the bar-end shifter into high gear and complete our Tour de Idaho in a little over 24 hours. It sounds impressive until you take a close look at a map.

Near Round Lake State Park we stopped to talk with two gentlemen cyclists who had started near Seattle. They had just got back "on route" after a wrong turn had cost them a 20 mile detour. We had the usually exchange of route tips, and learned that they would be finishing in Whitefish, Montana where they would be boarding Amtrak and paying all of $15 to transport their bikes back with them. We considered taking the train back home but the four day ride didn't appeal to us (maybe so if we could afford the sleeping berth).

In Newport, which was just inside the Washington State border (and yet there was no "Welcome to Washington" sign) we headed downtown and found Michael's Café for a late lunch. Later we camped at the "Hilton" of campgrounds, the Old American. For $16 we had a site, an outdoor hot tub, showers, laundry facilities, and some nice RV neighbors from British Columbia who put our two warm cans of beer in their freezer for an hour. They say good freezers make good neighbors . . . .

<u>Day 85, August 16, Newport to Ione, WA, 52 miles</u>
After ordering the "Big Breakfast" at McDonalds, Stephanie made the grave error of consuming one too many of those deep fried hockey pucks (a.k.a. "hash browns"). This would come back to haunt her just a couple miles out of town at the summit of "Hashbrown

Hill." If you hurry you may still see the remnants of the "historical marker."

That out of the way and Stephanie feeling better, we resumed our relatively level ride along the Pend Oreille River under cloudless blue skies. In the Kalispel Indian Reservation, we stopped at the Manressa Grotto, a large cave on a hillside overlooking the river. It was a meeting place for the Indians, still used to this day.

Now Stephanie had been regularly quoting three lines during our voyage, all originating from the big screen, to express her particular anguish of the moment. The first was, "I gotta eat!" from E.G. Marshall in National Lampoon's *Christmas Vacation*. This was usually blurted out about midday when the bacon wore off. The second was from the movie *Sandlot*, "You're killing me Smalls!" which she gasped at the top of a long tortuous climb. After a while I would respond to this one with, "Well, it sure is taking long enough! Shit! We're in (insert state here)!" Here at the Grotto, I borrowed her favorite (Scotty's from *Star Trek*), normally reserved for when a big hill came into sight. I had gone in to use the pit toilet, but as I ran out just seconds after entering (pinching my nose) I blurted out, "I just can't do it captain!"

By mid-afternoon we were in Ione where we feasted on burgers, chocolate cake, and coffee at the grocery store's food court. Later, while relaxing in our lawn chairs at Cedar Park Campground/Carwash, what we thought was one of the RV'ers passing gas turned out to be the spontaneous rupturing of our rear inner tube, our fifth and what would turn out to be our last flat tire.

## Day 86, August 17, Ione to Colville, WA, 38 miles

After a sumptuous breakfast at the Cabin diner outside of Ione, we began climbing the long series of switchbacks that would take us west out of the Pend Oreille watershed and into the valleys of the Columbia. This was just a warm up of what was looming ahead of us in the North Cascades. After going over the hump, we stopped at a general store by Lake Thomas. There we conversed with part of a group of a dozen "kid" cyclists (at 50 plus we were probably twice the age of the typical bike tourist). They were headed to Missoula, and they confessed of sleeping late and had stopped in for a quick breakfast of ice cream novelties.

We also stopped for pictures at the scenic overlook of Crystal Falls, a nice cool, shady cascade which gave us some relief from the increasingly hot afternoon.

Just outside of Colville we found Barry and Shelley's bike hostel, featuring a freezer stocked with three different flavors of ice cream (including "Tillamook Mudslide" which was my favorite). Showers, soft mattresses, a kitchen—and it was all free for cyclists. These guys rocked!

### Day 87, August 18, Colville to Boyds, WA, 26 miles

Today we had plans to attend one last Rotary meeting in Colville at noon. After Starbucks coffee and donuts for breakfast, we did some errands at the Colville post office and library. No visit to Colville would be complete without a stop at their awesome Laundromat, which draws the most domesticated men per capita in the world, thanks to the installation of several Pinball tables. But don't fret girls; their TV had a direct high-definition feed from the "Soap Opera" channel.

At Park Place Restaurant, we had a lively lunch with the fun-loving Rotary Club of Colville. Afterwards, we were treated to a presentation of some of the member's recent trip to India, where they helped vaccinate children for polio.

We finally were on the road by the middle of the afternoon, and later stopped at the Kettle Falls Historical Center (these actual "falls" of the Columbia River are now under several hundred feet of Lake Roosevelt's waters thanks to the Grand Coulee Dam). There we watched some vintage films showing the building of the dam, and the moving of the sacred Indian graves that would have been inundated by the new lake.

After crossing Lake Roosevelt, we had a decision to make: continue due west over Sherman and Wauconda Passes with a total of 6200' of elevation to climb, or detouring north over just one pass at Boulder Creek with 3200' of gain but in the process adding almost 15 miles to our route. We choose the latter.

Four miles into our detour we stopped for the night near Boyds at peaceful North Lake Roosevelt RV Park, our "base camp." We had been slackers today, and only covered 26 miles. But we were strategically within striking distance of Boulder Creek Pass, the first of four left between us and the Pacific.

## Day 88, August 19, Boyds to Curlew, WA, 35 miles

At Barstow, we stopped at what had to be the best stocked general store per cubic foot in all of the US of A. This guy had everything from wines to worms, composted chicken manure to Cappuccinos. We had a nice breakfast there on the cute little luncheonette counter.

At 4600', Boulder Creek Pass was not too high as passes go out west, but our climb started at 1400', so it was a tough twelve miles nonetheless. The road up the pass had little traffic and climbed up through a lush, green valley. A few miles shy of the summit, we had to stop and purify some water out of a stream as we were running low. Once at the top we took the celebratory photos, complete with our make-shift Tibetan prayer flags (our sweaty bandanas).

Next was a fast and furious eight mile downhill to Curlew, where we spent the night at The Cycle Camp and Breakfast, where Stephanie enjoyed her first "solar shower" in a little greenhouse (although she complained about the lack of privacy so I "MacGyvered" a towel door onto the shed).

## Day 89, August 20, Curlew to Tonasket, WA, 58 miles

We awoke to some very chilly temperatures, but got warmed up with a breakfast of hot oatmeal, muffins, and coffee brought out by our campground host. Soon we were on the road and flying along the Kettle River on our way to Wauconda. We stopped at the grave site of Ranald Macdonald, where he possibly succumbed from ingesting one too many of those Hashbrowns himself. Actually this Ranald lived back in the 1800's, and was best known for his adventures to Japan. At that time, the country was closed to outsiders, but he was so intrigued by the culture that he purposely "shipwrecked" himself close to the mainland from a whaling ship (after he invented the "McBlubber" of course) and was taken prisoner by the Japanese. In Japan he taught English for several years, before venturing on to Australia and eventually back to Washington State. We found this bit of local history very interesting, as our son Matt lives in Japan with his wife Emiko. They both teach English there. Matt was fortunate to have a high school (in New York State) that offered an "Eastern

Studies Program," which provided him a head start towards his mastery of the difficult Japanese language at Ohio State. Stephanie and I both agreed Ranald's visit to the Empire of the Rising Sun would have gone much smoother if only his high school had such a program.

Our turn south onto Toroda Creek Road came just four miles shy of the British Columbian border. This leg of our ride started innocently enough, with more good pavement, no traffic, and easy grades. However, about twelve miles from Wauconda the road turned to loose crushed stone—not much fun on a fully-loaded tandem even with our relatively wide 35 millimeter tires. Soon the grade steepened uphill and a headwind began to develop. We arrived at the Wauconda diner exhausted and starved.

After the great staff served us some tasty food, coffee, and dessert we decided to push on to Tonasket (another 24 miles but pretty much all downhill). As we descended, the countryside became more arid and rugged. We were on the dry eastern shadow of the Cascades.

We checked into the Corner Motel in Tonasket where, unfortunately, some rowdy contractors were staying as well. The party in the parking lot outside our door went on until midnight, complete with a guitar jam session.

### Day 90, August 21, Tonasket to Okanogan, WA, 33 mi (4014 miles total)

Today's highlight was surpassing the 4000 mile mark near Omak. Stephanie celebrated by shopping at Wal-Mart. I waited outside, making a few cell phone calls to check in with our children.

We arrived in Okanogan early in the afternoon and found the Taco Wagon, where Stephanie and I enjoyed an authentic Mexican soda and a "Superburrito." Judging by the crowd there and our taste buds, it was the best place to eat in town.

We were planning on continuing another ten miles to Leader Lake Campground, which would have partially broken up tomorrow's climb up Loup Loup Pass, until we learned the facility was without running water and that the lake was too skanky to swim in (it had been drawn down to irrigate the fruit farms in the valley). So we quit early and made camp at the Okanogan town park where the farmer's market had just finished up. Hard to pass on the flush toilets and showers! This made for a short day, but luckily I had a good book to read and Stephanie had her IPod fully charged to play Solitaire.

During my daily post-ride "spin check" of the wheels I discovered a little slop in the rear wheel bearings again, so we took the time to grease and readjust them with my cone wrenches. Voila! Ready for the last 200 miles.

Repacking the rear axle, note the plastic bag stretched out with tent stakes to catch the ball bearings.

## Day 91, August 22, Okanogan to Twisp, WA, 32 miles

We rode out of Okanogan bright and early, and after four and a half hours, 20 miles, 3200' of elevation gain, two bananas, four peanut butter cookies, three granola bars, one bag of cheesy rice crisps, a half pound of cheddar cheese, two applications of butt butter, and 120 ounces of water we reached the top of Loup Loup Pass. As we took photos by the sign announcing the summit, we discovered an inscribed rock left on the ground by another cyclist. On it was scratched a picture of a bicycle and the words "worth it right?"

It was cool and windy at the top, so we bundled up for the delightful eight mile, six percent grade downhill. During the descent we caught some great views of the North Cascades; their lofty peaks veiled in an approaching storm system from the Pacific.

**The North Cascades loom in the distance, just east of Twisp**

In no time we had checked in at the Blue Spruce Motel in Twisp, our reward for a job well done. We later walked into town for the fine Italian dinning at Tappi. With a name like "Twisp" we had high expectations for the town, and I must say it lived up to them.

On the way back to the hotel, we stopped at Hank's Market for a few items. While Stephanie spent 30 minutes picking out tomorrow's breakfast, I searched for a substitute for butt butter as we were getting low again. Right there in aisle seven I found it: "Udderly Smooth Udder Cream." I compared ingredients; almost identical! Some quick calculating in my head—hmmm, and at half the price per ounce.[6]

## Day 92, August 23, Twisp to Mazama, WA, 24 miles

Just outside of Winthrop, we enjoyed a great tour of the North Cascade Smokejumper Base with our smokejumper guide, a rookie named Blake. Besides showing us all the specialized equipment required to fight forest fires by parachuting out of aircraft, he told us the complete history of smokejumping, whose development occurred at this site back in the 1930's. At the onset of WWII, the experience gained was used to instruct the first paratroopers for the US Army. The base was pretty quiet today, as most of the smokejumpers were actually up in Canada, helping our neighbors to the north fight their fires.

We spent a few hours in very touristy Winthrop; its shops were like a merger between Frontiertown and Starbucks. Later at the town park, we slobbered over some very juicy local peaches while doing postcards (we hope they didn't arrive too sticky).

Again we took a short day mileage wise to set up a base camp in Mazama, making tomorrow's ascent up Washington and Rainy Passes (our last two) as short and painless as possible. There we found our gracious Warmshowers hosts Rob and Ina. They were fellow tandem riders who had completed a cross-country odyssey the summer before, traveling from Washington, DC back home with their two young children aboard. Unfortunately, we did not get to meet Ina; she was out backpacking with her son Wylie. While Rob cooked us a delicious pasta dinner we talked about all things tandem. We also

---

[6] By the following summer I had found a "cycling specific" Udder Cream manufactured by this company, at twice the price. Go figure.

learned that their daughter Maya was quite a promising cross-country skier, and we hoped that someday her talents bring them to Lake Placid's Olympic Trails so we could repay their hospitality.

## Day 93, August 24, Mazama to Diablo Lake, WA, 56 miles

"O! The Joy!"—William Clark, 1805

Now we knew how the Corps of Discovery felt when they were in reach of the Pacific! We couldn't have asked for a better day to cross the last of the passes; cool, sunny, and with a gentle tailwind. We met many other cyclists on the way up, all of who were traveling light and passing us, but yelling words of encouragement.[7]

**Admiring our progress during the ascent of Washington Pass**

---

[7]  Six months later, while spinning on a stationary bike at a gym in Lake Placid, I met Leisl, a luge athlete. After a short conversation, it occurred to us that she in fact had been one of the cheer-leading cyclists. Small world.

We slowly but steadily crept up the evergreen-cloaked U-shaped valley. Upon reaching the summit of Washington Pass, a great feeling of elation and relief came over Stephanie and me. Only after looking back and viewing the steep, twisting switchbacks from high atop the overlook did we realize what an impressive task we'd accomplished.

**Overlook, Summit of Washington Pass**

After a short col, we crested anti-climactic Rainy Pass—just a "pimple on the map," I told my wife (as viewed from the elevation profile). From there it was a scenic and seemingly endless downhill filled with views of glaciated peaks and turquoise colored lakes. The vegetation almost immediately became more lush and a deeper shade of green, having received all the moisture-laden weather coming off the Pacific Ocean.

During the descent we passed many loaded cyclists climbing from the west, and it was our turn to cheer them on. It was bittersweet; they were just beginning their adventure, and ours was coming to an end.

At the Colonial Campground at Diablo Lake Stephanie and I were overjoyed to see my brother David, who had driven a car from Seattle to meet and camp with us. This was the first familiar face we had seen since day one in Virginia when our friend Sherrill had met us for dinner. Dave had in his trunk cold beer, chocolate and the makings for a pasta dinner. Later we had a great evening around a campfire, Dave letting us to know just how proud he was of our accomplishments thus far.

On this relatively long day I had put the Udder Cream to the test, and found it passed with flying colors. I just hope I didn't develop nipples on my buttocks.

### Day 94, August 25, Diablo Lake to Darrington, WA, 54 miles

Firing up the campstove, Dave treated us to a great breakfast of blueberry pancakes. If that wasn't enough, he gave us snacks and fixings for lunch plus agreed to lighten our load by taking all of our camping gear with him in the car. We wouldn't need it again; one last night in a motel and if all went well we'd be at Dave and Lynn's in Seattle the next day.

**David**

We thanked Dave as he drove off, and headed down along the Skagit River to Newhalem. There we stopped at the North Cascades Visitor's Center, where we checked out the natural history exhibits and had a nice picnic lunch. We met a gentleman vacationing from Amsterdam, the Netherlands who was very interested in our tour and wished he was on a bike himself (cycling is a major form of transportation there).

Fourteen more miles west we found the junction of route 530, which took us south along the very cool, green and shady Sauk River valley. We were in Darrington before we knew it, one long day's ride from Seattle!

That night, Denise, our sister-in-law from Maryland commented on our blog:

> "I am jealous that you got pancakes homemade for you. Do I have to ride thousands of miles to get pancakes? Tell Chris to make me some! I hope you are very proud of yourselves—you deserve all the pancakes and delicious breakfasts. Only five flat tires. Did I read that right?— Love, Denise"

Her husband (my brother Chris) later commented:

> "What's all the congratulations stuff? Its two minutes left in the fourth quarter. Let's not have any premature champagne and start practicing the "I am going to Disneyland" speech just yet. Put on the game faces, slather up on the sun tan lotion and butt butter, shift her into high gear, and push her over the goal line and into the Emerald City! Then, I'll send my worthy congratulations. Anyway, I've got to go buy some pancake mix for my lovely wife." —Chris

## Day 95, August 26, Darrington to Seattle, WA, 80 miles

We got off to an early start from Darrington after a superb breakfast at the Glacier View Cafe (majestic Glacier Peak towers over the little town). Lynn had forecast some rain by midday so we were hoping to get a good part of the ride over before then.

We had the first 29 miles into Arlington covered by mid-morning but by the time we rolled onto the Centennial Rail Trail just south of town the drops began to fall. We arrived in bustling city of Everett very damp and chilled (despite our multiple layers of clothing and rain gear). As if an answer to our prayers the American Institution of Denny's appeared as we rounded an intersection. Stephanie ordered a bowl of steaming chicken noodle soup and we both took advantage of the bottomless mug of hot chocolate. Soon we were ready to face Mother Nature and Father Traffic again.

A few hours later the rain let up, and we found the entrance to the Burke-Gilman Bike Trail. As we headed down the west side of Lake Washington, I was soon comforted by the sight of familiar scenery, as I had taken day rides down this trail on previous visits to Seattle. Before long we spotted Dave, who had again come out to greet us, this time on his bike. We followed him the rest of the way to his home, where he took a few pictures of the two happy but very tired cyclists. After a hot shower and a nap, we walked down to a nearby restaurant where Dave and Lynn treated us to dinner to celebrate the 99.7% completion of our voyage.

**Elated but exhausted at Dave and Lynn's**

## Day 96, August 27, Seattle, WA, 0 miles

We slept in late until the alluring smell of coffee and more of Dave's delectable blueberry pancakes became too unbearable to resist. Later I gave the bike a well deserved sponge bath in the backyard (it's first of the trip). It was a beautiful day, so Stephanie and I walked down to a quiet, little sidewalk cafe where we bought a few dozen Seattle postcards. Relaxing out in the warm sunshine, we then began to write thank you notes to all the wonderful people we had met along the way who had made our ride so special.

Later that evening was our first of several family get-togethers in Seattle. Beside's Dave and Lynn and their three sons, I had another two brothers, a sister, their spouses, and several more nieces and another nephew in Seattle to visit. Stephanie and I were wined and dined and treated like royalty for several days until we flew out on the last day of the month.

## Day 97, August 28, Dave's to Puget Sound, WA, 11 miles (4271 miles grand total)

The grand finale! Under beautiful blue skies and ideal temperatures we rode mostly on the beautiful Seattle bike trail network down to the salty Pacific waters of Puget Sound, escorted by Dave and Lynn and my brother Pete.

At Golden Gardens boat launch we rolled the front wheel into the water, completing our transcontinental journey. However, the photo shoot was in jeopardy when a rude and impatience power boater insisted that he had to launch his boat at that very moment. Our only ugly moment with a motorist on the whole trip, and it involved a "share the road" controversy with a boat on the last ten feet of pavement! After a minute of storing some pixels on our cameras we were out of his way.

On our way back to Dave's house the celebration continued, first at the Canal Coffee Shop (after all—this was Seattle—the most caffeinated city in the world) and later at Ivar's Restaurant where Stephanie satisfied a craving for their famous clam chowder (most likely brought on by inhaling too much of the salty sea air).

**Still in love at the Pacific**

<u>August 29-31, Last Days in Seattle</u>

The next day I began dismantling the bike for shipping. UPS had given us an estimate of less than $200 to ship the tandem back to New York. Dave drove me down to one of many fine bike shops in town, where I was given two boxes from new single bikes, along with the cushioning material. Cutting off one end of each box, I slipped the two together for a custom fit. Fifty yards of strapping tape later, I was content that the package would remain intact for the return trip, which it did. My compliments to UPS. Total cost was less than $170, which included insurance.

On the morning of August 31, Stephanie and I boarded the SAME aircraft at Seattle-Tacoma International Airport for home, after 4271 miles of tandem bicycling. After the long flight was finally over, and as we carried our luggage through the airport in Albany, New York, I could only look back, and with a tear in my eye—say to Stephanie, "Somebody needs to invent a pannier that has wheels and a long slide out handle! My arms are killing me!"

The next day Stephanie's sister Jacqueline and her husband Patrick surprised us with a "homecoming" party, and we enjoyed our celebrity status amongst friends and family!

# EPILOGUE

Although it was extremely hard work, Stephanie and I already miss our days on the road. The beautiful yet diverse scenery that America has to offer and the daily encounters with all of the wonderful, sincere people were a joy we shall always cherish. The voyage was especially satisfying being self-propelled and at the slow pace of a bicycle. Every great view lasted that much longer!

Traveling in the relatively fragile mode of cycling, exposed to the weather and stress brought upon by its physical exertion, one is much more in need of finding the basic necessities of food, water and shelter, which in turn requires frequent interaction with communities and its inhabitants. This we found to be one of the most rewarding perks of traveling by bicycle.

It was also a great journey into America's past, to relive the westward expansion of our country by visiting all the historic sites, reading ALL of the historic markers, and traveling over some of the same trails and passes that the westward pioneers took. A colleague of mine, who followed our adventure on our daily blog, commented:

> "I've learned more about US geography in last three months than I did in all my years at school."
>
> Bill M

We also met, rode, dined and camped with cyclists of all ages, from all over the world, with which we will always feel a special bond, having shared in all the joys and hardships, laughs and tears that are all part of the bicycle touring experience.

And most important, my wife, Stephanie, and I did it as a team, through thick and thin, successfully completing and enjoying the biggest adventure of our lives next to raising our four wonderful children. After thirty years of marriage, there may have been an easier way to renew our wedding vows, but we wouldn't trade this experience for the world!